T0196912

The True Understanding Of The End-Times

Re: Israel and the Church

LANCE MORGAN

(NB: All scriptures are from the KJV unless otherwise noted).
[ ] words in these brackets are mine.

WESTBOW
PRESS®
A DIVISION OF THOMAS NELSON
& ZONDERVAN

WestBow Press books may be ordered through booksellers or by contacting:

WestBow Press
A Division of Thomas Nelson & Zondervan
1663 Liberty Drive
Bloomington, IN 47403
www.westbowpress.com
1 (866) 928-1240

Scripture taken from the King James Version of the Bible.

THE HOLY BIBLE, NEW INTERNATIONAL VERSION®,
NIV® Copyright © 1973, 1978, 1984, 2011 by Biblica, Inc.®
Used by permission. All rights reserved worldwide.

ISBN: 978-1-5127-5021-8 (sc)
ISBN: 978-1-5127-5020-1 (e)

Library of Congress Control Number: 2016911651

Print information available on the last page.

WestBow Press rev. date: 9/21/2016

Contents

Prologue

Praise the Lord, greetings in the name of our Lord and Saviour Jesus Christ. To God be the glory, the honour and the praise, with regards to this work.

I have read so many books on the End-times all trying to explain the way it is going to play out up to the rapture and beyond. I started my look at these books, writings, excerpts and other related commentaries in about mid- 2009. At the time of writing, May, 2015, I have come to my own conclusion and understanding, of the End-times, and will attempt to set it out as best as I can in this book. It is important to note that my understanding is mostly through several revelations of Jesus Christ, firstly, then by a proper understanding of the combination of all the various texts and other information that I was able to cover. However I am **VERY CONFIDENT** that this work is correct. It is also important to note that not everything will be made clear to us until we are actually in the time of the End, that is, the last seven (7) years, OR THE 70TH WEEK, which has two, three and a half (3 ½) years' time period running concurrently. The final 3 ½ years is known as the **Time of Jacob's Trouble (Jer. 30:7),** or **The Great Tribulation (Matt. 24:21).**

It is also important to point out that no study of the End-times can be done without encountering the question of where the rapture fits in - whether Pre-Tribulation, Mid-Tribulation, Post-Tribulation or Pre-Wrath, as some folks believe. I will therefore compare and contrast scriptures to show the timing of several events of the End-times, and this is after several years of careful study and some revelations by the Lord.

Therefore, I will start this discourse by looking at the Rapture and the Day of The Lord, because they are closely entwined, happening almost simultaneously, at the seventh trumpet. Indeed the seventh trumpet ushers in both with some scriptures such as **Dan. 12: 1c-2**, among others, having them occurring at the same time. I will look at whatever differences or similarities there are, in the terms Rapture and the Day of The Lord. Other topics will be discussed and explained, to aid in the true understanding of the end-times. Do note that the man who will become the antichrist will only become the antichrist at the 1260 day point of the Week, but will set up the Abomination of Desolation at 1230 days. He is still called the antichrist however, right throughout the book, to make reading simple and easy. Please take note of this and be not confused. Bless!

1 The Church and the Rapture

The term rapture is not written in the Bible, but according to Wikipedia.org, in Christian eschatology the **rapture** refers to the belief that either before, or simultaneously with, the <u>Second Coming</u> of Jesus Christ to earth, believers who have died will be raised and believers who are still alive and remain shall be caught up together with them (the resurrected dead believers) in the clouds to meet the Lord in the air. The concept has its basis in various interpretations of the biblical book of **1 Thessalonians (4:16-17),** and how it relates to interpretations of various other biblical passages, such as those from Second Thessalonians, the Gospel of Matthew, First Corinthians 15: 51-53, and the Book of Revelation.

However the question as to the timing of the rapture about when it will take place is greatly disagreed upon amongst Christians. There are four major beliefs that encompass the timing of the rapture, namely, Pre-Tribulation, Mid-Tribulation, Post-Tribulation or Pre-Wrath. First let me explain each belief and then see what the scripture clearly says, for it is the Bible that must speak in this matter. Christians of any of the above belief will tell you that it is the Bible that gives them their belief, but I have learnt that one scripture alone should not decide a position one way or the other. You must search the scriptures carefully to see if the Lord speaks on the subject matter elsewhere, before arriving at your position, for at **"the mouth of two witnesses, or** at **the mouth of three witnesses**, shall the matter be established," (**Deut. 19:15; see also Matt. 18:16 & 2 Cor. 13:1**). To strengthen that, the Bible also states in **2 Tim. 2:15**, "study to shew thyself approved unto God, a workman that needeth not to be ashamed, **rightly dividing the word of truth**." So you must make a diligent search of the Bible and then get the correct understanding through fasting and prayer, before you assume a position on a matter, for example, on baptism, or tongues talking (glossolalia) or the Sabbath.

Pre-Tribulation

The first position I will discuss is Pre-Tribulation. Here's what Wikipedia.org has to say on the matter: The pre-tribulation position advocates that the **rapture** will occur **before** the beginning of the **seven-year tribulation period**, while the second coming will occur at the end of the seven-year tribulation period. Pre-tribbers often describe the rapture as Jesus coming *for* the church and the second coming as Jesus coming *with* the church.

One immediate question arises, how many times will the Lord Jesus Christ come again or put another way, how many returns are there? We shall see when the Bible texts are used later on.

Mid-Tribulation

The Mid-Tribulation view holds that the **rapture** will take place during the middle of the tribulation period, that is, during the second 3 ½ years reign of the Antichrist. "The tribulation is typically divided into two periods of 3.5 years each. Mid-tribulationists hold that the saints will go through the first period (Beginning of Travail, which is not "the tribulation"), but will be raptured into Heaven before the severe outpouring of God's wrath in the second half of what is popularly called the Great Tribulation."

Post-Tribulation

Wikipedia.org states, "the post-tribulation position places the rapture at the end of the tribulation period. Post-tribulation writers define the tribulation period in a generic sense as the entire present age, or in a specific sense of a period of time preceding the second coming of Christ. The emphasis in this view is that the church will undergo the tribulation — even though the church will be spared the wrath of God. Matthew 24:29–31 - *"Immediately after the Tribulation of those days...they shall gather together his elect..."* - is cited as a foundational scripture for this view. Post-tribbers perceive the rapture as occurring simultaneously with the second coming of Christ. Upon Jesus' return, believers will meet him in the air and will then accompany him in his return to the Earth." **(THIS IS MY GENERAL VIEW BUT I HAVE SOME VARIATIONS, SO READ ON).**

Pre-wrath

"This view also places the rapture at some point during the tribulation period before the second coming. It holds that the tribulation of the church begins toward the end of the seven-year period, when the Antichrist is revealed in the temple. This latter half of the seven-year period [i.e. 3 1/2 years] is defined as the great tribulation, although the exact duration is not known. The tribulation will be cut short by the coming of Christ to deliver the righteous by means of the rapture, which will occur after specific events in Revelation, in particular after the sixth seal is opened and the sun is darkened and the moon is turned to blood. However, by this point many Christians will have been slaughtered as martyrs by the Antichrist. After the rapture will come God's seventh-seal wrath of trumpets and bowls. The Day of the Lord's wrath against the ungodly will follow for the remainder of the seven years."

What is the Bible's position on the Tribulation

Here, I must digress a little to deal with the specific issue of the tribulation. Here is what **Daniel** said on the matter in **9:24 & 27**; 24 **"Seventy weeks are determined upon thy people and upon thy holy city, to finish the transgression, and to make an end of sins, and to make reconciliation for iniquity, and to bring in everlasting righteousness, and to seal up the vision and prophecy, and to anoint the most Holy. 27"And he shall confirm the covenant with many for one week: and in the midst of the week he shall cause the sacrifice and the oblation to cease, and for the overspreading of abominations he shall make it desolate, even until the consummation, and that determined shall be poured upon the desolate."**

This is the first text on the matter. Daniel clearly points out that 70 Weeks [70 x 7= 490 yrs] are determined for Israel, to end transgression and sin, and to bring in everlasting righteousness. Sixty nine (69) Weeks or 483 yrs have gone, and prophecy scholars refer to the gap between the 69 and 70th Week as the Parenthesis. This gap is between Christ's first coming as the sacrificial Lamb of God (Saviour), that took away the sins of the world by His death and resurrection, and His second coming as Redeemer and King. The time count (which God had paused due to Christ's rejection by Israel), resumes with the final 70th Week when "he", [the antichrist], will confirm a covenant with many for one week (70th WEEK), i.e. for seven (7) years. In the middle of this 7 years period he will cause [I prefer force or by force], the sacrifice that the Jews will be doing at that time, to cease. This shows that the Jews will resume animal sacrifice at some point in time before the midway point of the Week/7 year period of time in question, and may indeed have their 3rd Temple built . He shall desolate the holy place, i.e. the 3rd Temple or that area of the Temple Mount site that the Altar will be set up on. The Jews have already built on Altar with stones form the river Jordan, along with other Temple sacred vessels, and the garments of the High Priests. Rabbis Yisrael Ariel, Chaim Richman and the others at the Temple Institute in Jerusalem are carrying on this work in preparation for the resumption of animal sacrifices et al, that were carried out according to the Torah (the first 5 books of the Old Testament). Until the consummation means until the appointed time that the 70th Week comes to an end. Daniel explains it even further:

And arms shall stand on his part, and they shall pollute the sanctuary of strength, and shall take away the daily sacrifice, and they shall place the abomination that maketh desolate. Dan.11:31. See also Ezek. 7:21-21.

The antichrist soldiers will be on Temple Mount to pollute the Temple, and here again he points out that the antichrist will take away [force], i.e. stop the resumed daily sacrifice and will place a likely stature or idol there. He again makes this point in chapter 12.

And from the time that the daily sacrifice shall be taken away, and the abomination that maketh desolate set up, there shall be a thousand two hundred and ninety days. Dan. 12:11.

However Daniel now adds more information. He now shows how many days will be left to the end of the Tribulation, after the abomination had been set up, i.e. 1290 days or 3 /12 years plus 30 days, [1260 + 30 days]. Jesus referred to this statement of Daniel about the abomination, in the gospels, in **Matt. 24: 15-16 & 20-21,** see also **Mk. 13:14-19 & Luke 21:20-24.** Also see **Timeline Chart** at chapter three of book. It is Jesus who connects what Daniel stated, that a period of Tribulation will occur near the time of the end. This also proves that this tribulation DOES NOT refer to Antiochus IV Epiphanes (175-164 BC), who desecrated the Jewish Temple in 168 BC, but points instead to another future, vile person, aka, the antichrist. Here's Jesus' take on the matter in Matt. 24.

When ye therefore shall see the <u>abomination of desolation</u>, spoken of by Daniel the prophet, stand in the holy place, (whoso readeth, let him understand:).

Then let them which be in Judaea flee into the mountains: …..

But pray ye that your flight be not in the winter, neither on the sabbath day:

For then shall be <u>great tribulation</u>, such as was not since the beginning of the world to this time, no, nor ever shall be. Matt. 24: 15-16 & 20-21.

So it is the final <u>1260</u> days that will be the **great tribulation,** with the 30 days prior to then being the last period that the Jews will have to flee for their lives. However many will not take heed to the prophecy and will remain, and thus will be killed by the antichrist, by famine and pestilences and sold into slavery. I will come back to this later on.

This same time period of great tribulation is what Jeremiah called the **time of Jacob's trouble,** so stated because I believe Jeremiah used the word Jacob to show it was all of Israel that would be attacked/punished. Thus he did not use the word Israel lest anyone mistook him to mean the Tribes of Judah and Benjamin as different from the separated ten tribes. This separation occurred at the time of Solomon and Jeroboam in **1 Kings 11**, see **v 31**. The actual split took place during the reign of Solomon's son, Rehoboam. See the rest of the story in the following chapters after **chap 11**. So Jeremiah used the word Jacob showing that it will be all OF THE TRIBES that will be punished by God, at the hands of the antichrist. Here is the text: **Jer. 30:5-7.**

For thus saith the Lord; We have heard a voice of trembling, of fear, and not of peace. Ask ye now, and see whether a man doth travail with child? wherefore do I see every man with his hands on his loins, as a woman in travail, and all faces are turned into paleness?

Alas! for that day is great, so that none is like it: it is even the <u>time of Jacob's trouble</u>, but he shall be saved out of it.

Later on the Lord revealed more to John the Apostle in the book of **Revelation 6: 9-11.**

⁹ And when he had opened the fifth seal, I saw under the altar the souls of them that were slain for the word of God, and for the testimony which they held:¹⁰ And they cried with a loud voice, saying, How long, O Lord, holy and true, dost thou not judge and avenge our blood on them that dwell on the earth?

¹¹ And white robes were given unto every one of them; and it was said unto them, that they should rest yet for a little season, until their fellowservants also and their brethren, that should be killed as they were, should be fulfilled.

Here is John stating that many saints will and must be killed in this period of tribulation. I believe this will happen in other countries apart from Israel. Certainly the tribulation will affect Christians, who will be persecuted and tested worldwide, for their faith in Christ.

See the tribulation below being touched upon in **Rev. 12: 14-17,** as it relates to Christians.

¹⁴ And to the woman were given two wings of a great eagle, that she might fly into the wilderness, into her place, where she [Israel] is nourished for a time, and times, and half a time, from the face of the serpent.¹⁵ And the serpent cast out of his mouth water as a flood after the woman, that he might cause her to be carried away of the flood.

¹⁶ And the earth helped the woman, and the earth opened her mouth, and swallowed up the flood which the dragon cast out of his mouth.¹⁷ And the dragon was wroth with the woman, and went to make war with the remnant of her seed, which keep the commandments of God [Israel], and have the testimony of Jesus Christ [the Church].

This time [1yr] and times [2yrs], and half a time [6 months], corresponds to the said 1260 days or 3 ½ years' time period stated by the prophet Daniel. Notice that the serpent, through the antichrist is seen attacking those who escape from Jerusalem but that they are helped by the earth [i.e. by God's agents, angels??] to escape into a safe place [the wilderness]. The time period, you guessed it, the said 1260 days. So where as some escape him, the serpent then turns his attention to the remnant. This remnant contrary to popular belief cannot be Jews alone, for Jews as a nation do not believe in Jesus

Christ as God, but Jehovah as God in the faith of Judaism ...so it has to be inclusive of <u>both</u> sets of people. This must be why the Apostle John uses the terms **"which keep the commandments of God"** [denoting the Jews], **"and have the testimony of Jesus Christ" [Christians], so I believe it really means both.** It is important that I point out here a very key fact. In the body of Christ, i.e., within the Church, will be Jews and Gentiles, for there is no difference where Christ is concerned, all are one.

²⁷ **For as many of you as have been baptized into Christ have put on Christ.** ²⁸ **There is neither Jew nor Greek, there is neither bond nor free, there is neither male nor female: for ye are all one in Christ Jesus. Gal. 3: 27-28.** (See also **Col. 3: 11**).

So for me, the antichrist will then be attacking all those who profess faith in God, whether they be Jews or Gentiles in this 1260 day tribulation period. For you see, he will be demanding via the false prophet that he is the one to be worshipped as God. This is touched upon in **chap 13: 5 -10,** and here again is John speaking of the antichrist in the tribulation period.

⁵ **And there was given unto him a mouth speaking great things and blasphemies; and power was given unto him to continue <u>forty and two months</u>.**

⁶ **And he opened his mouth in blasphemy against God, to blaspheme his name, and his tabernacle, and them that dwell in heaven.**⁷ **And it was given unto him to make war with the saints, and to overcome them: and power was given him over all kindreds, and tongues, and nations.**

⁸ **And all that dwell upon the earth shall worship him, whose names are not written in the book of life of the Lamb slain from the foundation of the world.**

⁹ **If any man have an ear, let him hear.**¹⁰ **He that leadeth into captivity shall go into captivity: he that killeth with the sword must be killed with the sword. Here is the patience and the faith of the saints.**

Following on from chap 6 & 12, John points out here that even though many saints will be killed during the forty and two months

[1260 days] or [3 ½ yrs], by the antichrist and his soldiers, the saints must exercise patience. For those who will be made captive, will be made captive; and those who will die by the sword, will die likewise. Notice that, "**all that dwell upon the earth shall worship him, whose names are not written in the book of life of the Lamb slain from the foundation of the world.**" Indeed v 12 states,

[12] And he exerciseth all the power of the first beast before him, and causeth the earth and them which dwell therein to worship the first beast, whose deadly wound was healed.

John continues talking about the worshipping of the antichrist:

[13] And he doeth great wonders, so that he maketh fire come down from heaven on the earth in the sight of men, [14] And deceiveth them that dwell on the earth by the means of those miracles which he had power to do in the sight of the beast; saying to them that dwell on the earth, that they should make an image to the beast, which had the wound by a sword, and did live.

[15] And he had power to give life unto the image of the beast, that the image of the beast should both speak, and cause that as many as would not worship the image of the beast should be killed. [16] And he causeth all, both small and great, rich and poor, free and bond, to receive a mark in their right hand, or in their foreheads: [17] And that no man might buy or sell, save he that had the mark, or the name of the beast, or the number of his name.

[18] Here is wisdom. Let him that hath understanding count the number of the beast: for it is the number of a man; and his number is Six hundred threescore and six.

Here is the worship of the antichrist, indeed a statue is built of him, by the false prophet, which all those who do not bow down and worship, then they will be killed. It is important to point out though, that it is those whom the antichrist, via his agents, can catch. If a person is caught and having been commanded to bow down and worship the beast [for the image represents him], and does not obey, then torture and death, likely by beheading will follow. Consider the three Hebrew men, and also the man Daniel, in the lion's den, challenged and persecuted because of their steadfast faith. I believe in some cases that persons will be tortured to change their belief in the One True God, Jesus Christ, before the death penalty be applied. In this tribulation time, you see then, why John points out "**here is the patience of the saints**. The tribulation period will test and prove those of us who are alive then, how much we really love the Lord. Take the mark and you can eat and drink, or not be tortured; refuse, and you suffer. You may also have to go without food for a day or two until God provides, or go where God sends you in order that you may be safe from the agents of the antichrist. There you will be provided for, consider Elijah and the ravens; consider also, those who flee Jerusalem and other Israeli cities from the antichrist to the wilderness. Consider also that there will be parents who will betray their children to the antichrist soldiers and agents, and likewise children betraying parents. A brother will betray his sister and vice versa, indeed friends and families will turn on one another. Jesus speaks of this in **Matt. 24:10,**

[10] **And then shall many be offended, and shall betray one another, and shall hate one another.**

You are therefore pre-warned of what will happen in those days, to God be the glory, Blessed be HE. Therefore, in conclusion, the great tribulation is 1260 days, 42 months or 3 ½ years of persecution against all of God's people by the antichrist. It will be against the Jews in Israel [Jacob's trouble] and out of Israel; it will also be against all Christians [saints] everywhere across the entire world. Which is partly why there will be a great falling away as written by the Apostle Paul, and why Jesus warned "many false prophets shall rise, and shall deceive many." I will speak more on this matter when I get to the topic of the antichrist. This leads me to my next topic which just further proves my point.

In the meantime here are more great tribulation texts for further reading, please read them:

Dan.8:9-14 & 23-25; 11:31-45; Dan. 12:11-12; Hab. 1:1-11; Isa. 10:5-14 & 24-27; Zech.14 :2b-2c; Joel 3:1-6; Ezek. 6; and Rev. chaps 6 -18.

The controversy

I must pause here to comment on the great controversy in Christianity on the matter of the words **"elect"** and to a lesser extent, **"saints"**. Be reminded that we are still on the matter of the rapture, but these sub-topics are crucial for the proper understanding of the rapture.

The great controversy holds that the word **"elect"** as used in **Matt. 24:22**, is speaking solely of the Jews, or in other words, this word and passage is ONLY referring to the JEWS. This is not so and I will prove it here. In referring to the great tribulation, Jesus continued by saying:

²² And except those days should be shortened, there should no flesh be saved: but for the elect's sake those days shall be shortened.

It is very interesting to hear Christian leaders argue that Jesus was talking to the Jews only. In fact Jesus spoke these words to his disciples on the Mount of Olives. Here it is, so let's examine the passage to see if it was only for the Jews.

³ And as he sat upon the mount of Olives, the disciples came unto him privately, saying, Tell us, when shall these things be? and what shall be the sign of thy coming, and of the end of the world? ⁴ And Jesus answered and said unto them, Take heed that no man deceive you. Matt. 24:3-4.

So it is clear who Jesus spoke to - his disciples, who were Jews. These same disciples however, later on became the starting point for the church. They were numbered among the 120 people (**Acts 1:15**) who were in the upper room on the day of Pentecost in Jerusalem. So there is no controversy here, it's the same disciples. It is plain to see that Jesus spoke to his disciples who represented a duality of purpose.

They represent for the Church (being under grace), but also for the nation of Israel, as they were Jews by birth, and thus the Bible said, **"for salvation is of the Jews." (Jn.4:22).** It follows for the Jews have the adoption, and the glory, and the covenants, and the giving of the law, and the service of God, and the promises**; Rom.9:4.** How can we not see that the church is definitely involved? The disciples started the church (by Christ), along with the others of the 120, and they were the same disciples Jesus spoke to in Matt 24. **This text – i.e. Matt.24 - is one clue that the tribulation will include both the church and the nation of Israel.** Interestingly, notice the question asked of Jesus in **Matt. 24: "Tell us, when shall these things be? and what shall be the sign of thy coming, and of the end of the world?"** It is clear the disciples were referring to the second coming of the Lord Jesus Christ. This also confirms that this passage was and is also very much for the Church, not just for the Jews. For Christ returns for the church at HIS second coming. Why do people misinterpret this? **Acts 2:47b** then stated nicely: …. "And the Lord added to the church daily such as should be saved."

Thus in answering the disciples' questions of **Matt. 24: 3,** Jesus' answers included **v 22** above which uses the word **"elect". It DOES NOT REFER TO THE JEWS ALONE.** The word **elect** comes from the Greek word **Ekletos** (Strong Exhaustive Concordance Bible), which means to select, chosen. This word is repeatedly used in the New Testament by all the writers and in its purest form means chosen ones. We the children of God, are chosen by HIM. **Eph. 1:4** says: **"According as he hath chosen us in him before the foundation of the world."** That's all there is to it, all Christians are chosen by God, so too were those men of the Old Testament, like Abel, Abraham, Isaac, Jacob, Moses, Elijah, Elisha, Daniel and many others including women like Ruth and Deborah. So **it does not refer to the Jews alone**, but all who are chosen by God from creation to the present and for the future until the rapture, will become a part of the elect, there is neither Jew nor Greek, bond or free, male or female, for all are one in Christ Jesus (**Gal. 3:28**). Observe these scriptures which clearly shows the church members being called the **elect**:

Put on therefore, <u>as the elect of God</u>, holy and beloved, bowels of mercies, kindness, humbleness of mind, meekness, longsuffering; <u>Col. 3:12.</u>

Paul, a servant of God, and an apostle of Jesus Christ, according to the faith of <u>God's elect</u>, and the acknowledging of the truth which is after godliness; <u>Titus 1:1.</u>

1 Peter, an apostle of Jesus Christ, to the strangers scattered throughout Pontus, Galatia, Cappadocia, Asia, and Bithynia, [2]<u>Elect</u> according to the foreknowledge of God the Father, through sanctification of the Spirit, unto obedience and sprinkling of the blood of Jesus Christ: Grace unto you, and peace, be multiplied. <u>1 Peter 1: 1-2.</u>

All arguments done. No more controversy. These texts prove that the word elect is referring to those of us chosen by God, not specifically Jews, for the church consists of Jews and Gentiles and in these cases, the Apostles are talking to those in the church. Almost all usage in the New Testament speaks of the church, not to the Jews in of themselves.

Now I move to the next word, **"saints"**. The usage of this word basically means a holy one, and this is both true of the Old and New Testament. In the New Testament, the Greek word **Hagios** (Strong Exhaustive Concordance Bible), is used in **all** passages, while the Hebrew (Aramaic) word **Qaddis** is used in the Old Testament in many instances. However since Daniel and then John in **Revelation 13:7** uses the word in conjunction with the time of the antichrist, and it still means a holy one, then it points right back to these holy ones being the elect. This is almost synonymous therefore, for you have to be holy to be a part of the elect, and scripture says so, **"Be ye holy; for I am holy" 1 Pet. 1:16.** Let's compare a text of both writers:

[21] I beheld, and the same horn made war with the <u>saints,</u> and prevailed against them;

[22] Until the Ancient of days came, and judgment was given to the saints of the most High; and the time came that the saints possessed the kingdom. Dan.7:21-22.

[24] And his power shall be mighty, but not by his own power: and he shall destroy wonderfully, and shall prosper, and practise, and shall destroy the mighty and the holy people. Dan. 8:24.

Apostle John states:

[7] And it was given unto him to make war with the saints, and to overcome them: and power was given him over all kindreds, and tongues, and nations. Rev. 13:7.

Some will say Daniel spoke specifically to the Jews but not so, just observe **v 22**, the same **"saints possessed the kingdom".** This is the Kingdom of God prepared for his elect. Observe that John also used the word **saints** when speaking of the beast's attack on God's people. Look at **Dan. 12: 2,** "And many of them that sleep in the dust of the earth shall awake, some to everlasting life, and some to shame and everlasting contempt." Compare this with **1 Thess. 4:19-17.**

[16] For the Lord himself shall descend from heaven with a shout, with the voice of the archangel, and with the trump of God: and the dead in Christ shall rise first:

[17] Then we which are alive and remain shall be caught up together with them in the clouds, to meet the Lord in the air: and so shall we ever be with the Lord.

Praise the Lord, oh glory! This is the elect being raptured, those dead in Christ and those who are alive at HIS return. Bap bap! the case is closed. No more arguments or controversy. Both writers foresaw the rapture of God's elect, Jews and gentiles, male and female, bond and free. The word refers **not to Jews alone.** What, do we think that the Jews (whose religion is Judaism) will obey Jesus when they see the Abomination of desolation on Temple Mount? I tell you no, they (most) will instead stay and fight to defend it. I will prove this later on when I speak on the personage of the antichrist and I will also show the antichrist's route to Jerusalem. Few Judaistic Jews (Orthodox,

Reform or Conservative) will take heed to Matt. 24 et al, for they do not pay much attention to the New Testament but to the Torah with all its various rites and rituals. Instead it will be the Christian Jews, maybe few Judaistic Jews and Gentile Christians who will be in Israel, who will flee when they see the Abomination, as they will know of and take heed to the prophecy and warning of Jesus Christ. Few Jews will take heed, which will lead to a massacre. This coming massacre of the Jews will be discussed later.

Now for the icing on the cake to conclude the argument on the rapture, as also its timing. When I began studying the prophecies re the end-times, I started in the gospels from Matthew 24 and eventually came to **2 Thess. 2:1-3.** In fact I was really studying the antichrist personage, who I will discuss in the next chapter, and came to **2 Thess.,** when it struck me that the question of the rapture is intertwined with the matter of the antichrist. From the gospels, Jesus clearly pointed out that HIS return will be **after the tribulation.** This did not bother me as at that time I held to the pre-tribulationist view of the rapture. I had heard so many preachers say the Lord is coming soon and we should make sure we are ready that we do not miss the rapture for there would be serious consequencies. For sure the Lord is coming soon, and there will be very serious everlasting consequencies, if you miss the rapture. The everlasting consequencies also holds true if you die without being saved, or be one of those who take the mark of the beast, before HE returns. However I did not fully understand the matter of the tribulation and of its timing. So here I was looking into the personage of the antichrist, when I came upon **2 Thess. 2:1-3:**

1 Now we beseech you, brethren, <u>by the coming of our Lord Jesus Christ, and by our gathering together unto him,</u>

² That ye be not soon shaken in mind, or be troubled, neither by spirit, nor by word, nor by letter as from us, as that <u>the day of Christ is</u> at hand.

³ Let no man deceive you by any means<u>: for that day shall not come, except there come a falling away first, and that man of sin be revealed, the son of perdition;</u>

So having the pre-trib belief and reading from the gospels, I simply could not balance the equation, so to speak. That is, the rapture's timing and pre-trib belief did not match up with what Paul was saying in **2 Thess. 2**. You see I had not fully understood my reading of Jesus' words in the gospels (Matt. 24, Mk. 13 & Luke 21). So I was confused. I recall so many messages saying the rapture is next and soon, and that the church will not be here during the tribulation. So even though Jesus clearly has the rapture occurring **after the tribulation,** the church's teaching is that it was to the Jews that Jesus was talking and therefore it was not for the church. The church would be long gone from the scene. Well I have already shown so far that this is not so. Jesus by talking to the disciples, referenced both Jews and the Church. Moreover here was Paul speaking to the saints at Thessolonica (Jews? I think not), that "Let no man deceive you by any means: <u>for that day shall not come, except there come a falling away first, and that man of sin be revealed, the son of perdition;</u>" This is **SO CLEAR. THE RETURN OF CHRIST CANNOT HAPPEN UNTIL <u>AFTER</u>** the man of sin [the antichrist] is revealed.

Paul was very clear. He was speaking about the coming of the Lord and our gathering together unto him. **IS THIS NOT THE RAPTURE DEAR FRIENDS, HELLOOO**! So Paul said the rapture or day of Christ [also called day of the Lord elsewhere], **shall not come until we see the antichrist.** That is what he is actually saying here. As soon as I accepted Paul's position, my 'vision' cleared. NO MORE CONFUSION. It hit me hard. **The realization hit me that the church, yes the church, will be in the tribulation,** because I had by then read a lot about the antichrist and his subsequent actions on earth. Once this message settled in my mind, a whole lot of other scriptures suddenly became clear to me. The equation became balanced. The church would go through the tribulation because the antichrist would reign for 1260 days/42 months or 3 ½ years. Note however, <u>that it is not at the same time the antichrist is revealed or a little time after, say a few days or months or a year, that the rapture would occur</u>. No, but **after** the set time of **3 ½ years of tribulation**, plus some more days, that the rapture would occur. In this tribulation period (the 70th Week), in the first period of 3 ½ years before the Abomination, the falling away will begin and get worse during the great tribulation (the last 3 ½ yrs). I will prove all of this shortly. Consider what Jesus said in entirety in **Matt. 24: 29-31**.

[29] Immediately [very soon after] after the tribulation of those days shall the sun be darkened, and the moon shall not give her light, and the stars shall fall from heaven, and the powers of the heavens shall be shaken:

[30] And then shall appear the sign of the Son of man in heaven: and then shall all the tribes of the earth mourn, and they shall see the Son of man coming in the clouds of heaven with power and great glory.

[31] And he shall send his angels with a great sound of a trumpet, and they shall gather together his elect from the four winds, from one end of heaven to the other.

Compare **Mark 13:24-27**.

[24] But in those days, after that tribulation, the sun shall be darkened, and the moon shall not give her light, [25] And the stars of heaven shall fall, and the powers that are in heaven shall be shaken.

[26] And then shall they see the Son of man coming in the clouds with great power and glory. [27] And then shall he send his angels, and shall gather together his elect from the four winds, from the uttermost part of the earth to the uttermost part of heaven.

See also **Luke 21:25-28**.

[25] And there shall be signs in the sun, and in the moon, and in the stars; and upon the earth distress of nations, with perplexity; the sea and the waves roaring;

[26] Men's hearts failing them for fear, and for looking after those things which are coming on the earth: for the powers of heaven shall be shaken.

[27] And then shall they see the Son of man coming in a cloud with power and great glory. [28] And when these things begin to come to pass, then look up, and lift up your heads; for your redemption draweth nigh.

Those are Jesus' words. HE clearly states that HIS return for the elect will be **after** the tribulation of those days, in other words, **it's after the great tribulation.** All the tribes of the earth (all people) **shall see** HIM at HIS return, and shall mourn – these are those who are not ready to meet HIM. The prospect of eternal damnation suddenly looms large as they will see that they were worshipping the wrong 'saviour' – the antichrist. Those who are looking for HIS return – the elect - will be rejoicing though, for our trials and temptations will be over. Notice that there is a trumpet sounded, that the angels gather the elect from all over the earth, not just from Israel. Do you still disbelieve, well it gets more interesting, as other writers confirm Jesus' words. Look at what John said in **Revelation 1:7.**

[7] **Behold, he cometh with clouds; and every eye shall see him, and they also which pierced him: and all kindreds of the earth shall wail because of him. Even so, Amen.**

He said the very same thing. At Jesus' return, all eyes shall see HIM, even them who pierced HIM (the Jews), and there will be wailing (mourning) at that time. Jesus' return will **NOT BE SECRET.** All eyes shall behold HIM, but whereas the elect will rejoice, the reject will mourn. **Dan. 12:2** says: **And many of them that sleep in the dust of the earth shall awake, some to everlasting life, and some to shame and everlasting contempt.** Here is Daniel basically saying the same thing. Some of the dead shall awake to eternal life (rejoicing), whilst some will mourn owing to the shame and eternal contempt, when they awake after the Millennium. It's the same GOD WHO IS COMING BACK, not another. There are yet more texts to prove the return is after the tribulation. Here's Joel take on the matter.

[30] **And I will shew wonders in the heavens and in the earth, blood, and fire, and pillars of smoke.** [31] **The sun shall be turned into darkness, and the moon into blood, before the great and terrible day of the Lord come. Joel 3:30-31.**

He agrees with Matthew, Mark and Luke. Look at the common words: moon turns into blood, sun into darkness and stars fall from

<u>heaven, and the powers of the heavens shaking</u>. The Apostles **all** say it's **after the tribulation** that these signs occur. They concur with Joel that it is after these signs that the Lord will return for the elect, but notice that Joel calls the time **the day of the Lord.** HOW VERY INTERESTING INDEED. Do you see this? **The return happens on the day of the Lord, after the various signs, and is also after the tribulation.** But stand still, there are yet more writers on this topic. Let's view them:

¹² Let the heathen be wakened, and come up to the valley of Jehoshaphat: for there will I sit to judge all the heathen round about.¹³ Put ye in the sickle, for the harvest is ripe: come, get you down; for the press is full, the fats overflow; for their wickedness is great.

¹⁴Multitudes, multitudes in the valley of decision: for <u>the day of the Lord</u> is near in the valley of decision.¹⁵ The sun and the moon shall be darkened, and the stars shall withdraw their shining.

¹⁶ The Lord also shall roar out of Zion, and utter his voice from Jerusalem; and the heavens and the earth shall shake: but the Lord will be the hope of his people, and the strength of the children of Israel. <u>Joel 3:12-16.</u>

¹⁴ The <u>great day of the Lord</u> is near, it is near, and hasteth greatly, even the voice of the day of the Lord: the mighty man shall cry there bitterly.

¹⁵ That day is a day of wrath, a day of trouble and distress, a day of wasteness and desolation, a day of darkness and gloominess, a day of clouds and thick darkness,¹⁶ A day of the trumpet and alarm against the fenced cities, and against the high towers. <u>Zeph. 1:14-16.</u>

⁹ Behold, <u>the day of the Lord</u> cometh, cruel both with wrath and fierce anger, to lay the land desolate: and he shall destroy the sinners thereof out of it.

¹⁰ For the stars of heaven and the constellations thereof shall not give their light: the sun shall be darkened in his going forth, and the moon shall not cause her light to shine.¹¹ And I will punish the world for their evil, and the wicked for their iniquity; and I will cause the arrogancy of the proud to cease, and will lay low the haughtiness of the terrible. <u>Isa 13:9-11.</u> Or read from v 1-13.

Lance Morgan

Consider Peter's take on the matter:

[10] But <u>the day of the Lord</u> will come as a <u>thief</u> in the night; in the which the heavens shall pass away with a great noise, and the elements shall melt with fervent heat, the earth also and the works that are therein shall be burned up.

[11] Seeing then that all these things shall be dissolved, what manner of persons ought ye to be in all holy conversation and godliness,[12] Looking for and hasting unto the coming of the day of God, wherein the heavens being on fire shall be dissolved, and the elements shall melt with fervent heat? <u>2 Pet. 3:10-12.</u>

Now here is Peter introducing a new term in describing the coming of the Lord, and notice he also called it the **day of the Lord**. This new term is the word **thief**. Here are a few texts that speak about this.

For yourselves know perfectly that the day of the Lord so cometh as <u>a thief</u> in the night. 1 Thess. 5:2

But ye, brethren, are not in darkness, that that day should overtake you as <u>a thief</u>. 1 Thess. 5: 4

Remember therefore how thou hast received and heard, and hold fast, and repent. If therefore thou shalt not watch, I will come on thee <u>as a thief</u>, and thou shalt not know what hour I will come upon thee. Rev. 3:3.

[15] Behold, I come as a <u>thief</u>. Blessed is he that <u>watcheth</u>, and keepeth his garments, lest he walk naked, and they see his shame. <u>Rev. 16:15.</u>

So there it is. The writers (Peter & John), said the Lord will return as a thief in the night, meaning like a thief coming unexpectedly in the night to steal a householders' belongings. He catches the householder unawares. Notice John in Revelation said the elect/saints should be watching for HIS return. Jesus also said this many times; **Luke 21:36 & Mark 13:35-37**. So just as how some folks will rejoice at His appearing, and some will mourn; so too must the elect be watching, not sleeping, so that they will not be caught unawares. The day of the Lord should therefore not catch the elect as a thief (as a surprise), but it is those who are not expecting HIM, that will be caught by surprise.

Here are other day of the Lord texts: Joel 2:1-11; Isa. 34:1-10; Mal. 4:1-3; Zech. 12:1-9, & 14: and the Gog war of Ezek. 39. I will get to the Revelation texts later as they are many. Now I will close this rapture issue with these few important scriptures.

[15] For this we say unto you by the word of the Lord, that we which are alive and remain unto the coming of the Lord shall not prevent them which are asleep.

[16] For the Lord himself shall descend from heaven with a shout, with the <u>voice of the archangel, and with the trump of God:</u> and the dead in Christ shall rise first:

[17] Then we which are alive and remain shall be caught up together with them in the clouds, to meet the Lord in the air: and so shall we ever be with the Lord. <u>1 Thess. 4:15-17</u>

and

[51] Behold, I shew you a <u>mystery;</u> We shall not all sleep, but we shall all be changed,

[52] In a moment, in the twinkling of an eye, <u>at the last trump:</u> for the trumpet shall sound, and the dead shall be raised incorruptible, and we shall be changed. [53] For this corruptible must put on incorruption, and this mortal must put on immortality. <u>1 Cor. 15:51-53.</u>

and

[7] But in the days of the voice of the seventh angel, when he shall begin to sound, the <u>mystery</u> of God should be finished, as he hath declared to his servants the prophets. <u>Rev. 10:7</u>

[15] And the <u>seventh angel sounded;</u> and there were great voices in heaven, saying, The kingdoms of this world are become the kingdoms of our Lord, and of his Christ; and he shall reign for ever and ever.

[16] And the four and twenty elders, which sat before God on their seats, fell upon their faces, and worshipped God, [17] Saying, We give thee thanks, O Lord God Almighty, which art, and wast, and art to come; because thou hast taken to thee thy great power, and hast reigned.

¹⁸ And the nations were angry, and thy wrath is come, and the time of the dead, that they should be judged, and that thou shouldest give reward unto thy servants the prophets, and to the saints, and them that fear thy name, small and great; and shouldest destroy them which destroy the earth.

¹⁹ And the temple of God was opened in heaven, and there was seen in his temple the ark of his testament: and there were lightnings, and voices, and thunderings, and an earthquake, and great hail. <u>Rev. 11:15-19.</u>

Having taken you from what/when is the tribulation, showing that the **day of the Lord/ day of Christ**, and the **rapture** all coincide at a point, I will now give you the consummation. From the above scriptures we see that the Lord returns with a shout, after a **trumpet sounds.** Both Paul and John refer to it as a mystery, both say it will occur at the last trumpet. For even though Paul alone uses the words **"last trumpet"**, John says it's when the **seventh trumpet sounds. I put it to you that it's one and the same trumpet.** How could Paul know it would be the last trumpet that the return would take place except that God revealed it to him? How would Paul know (except by God's revelation), that of all the trumpet plagues to be revealed to John, it's at the last one that the mystery of God would be finished, that the kingdoms of this world would become the kingdoms of our Lord Jesus Christ, and HIS servants (prophets, saints - all God's people) would be rewarded. Is not this the rapture my friends? Not only that, HE will destroy those who are destroying the earth (this is Armageddon). This is the war that takes place in Ezek. 39, or in Rev. 19. Just view the identical terminology of flesh of kings, and the flesh of captains of mighty men, and the flesh of horses, and of them that sit on them, and the flesh of all men, both free and bond, prepared for birds to eat, that is used in both texts. All that remains is to show the fine line of timing from when the rapture takes place to the eventual Armageddon war, and this I will show later. But it all takes place on the day of the Lord, both the rapture and the battle of Armageddon. Thank God for HIS revelation.

Dessert

Here's some more food for thought. Why do pre-tribbers believe so much in the pre-trib rapture at the expense of the post-trib belief. Why say that God would not allow HIS people to go through tribulation. Didn't HE allow the Jews to be in Goshen, in Egypt whilst HE rained down all of ten plagues on the Egyptians. Hellooo? Did the Jews experience the plagues themselves, I tell you no. In fact even the very last plague, the killing of the first born, God used HIS supernatural power to deliver the Jews courtesy of the lamb slain and its blood put on the lintel of the doors. Now you tell me if this is not God raining down tribulation on them that trouble HIS people, while HIS people were present. Is it a far cry for us to be here and this time endure some tribulation for Christ, who suffered and died on Calvary's cross for us? After all, are we not at a higher plane than then? For this is the period of Grace (the Spirit), versus that period of the Law (the Letter). Bear in mind that those who are in Jerusalem are told to flee when they see the Abomination of Desolation, to a place prepared for them in the wilderness where they will be protected from the antichrist (does Goshen ring a bell?). You had better start preparing for that time, should you be around, for many Christians I tell you will join the antichrist when the Week begins, much more when the great tribulation begins. They will sell their soul for a morsel of bread, they will also sell out their fathers, mothers, siblings, other family members and friends. Many will be shocked to see the antichrist in action and yet they, as part of the church, are still here. Disbelieve at your peril.

Next, consider the scriptures below of first, Galatians chap. 3. Here Paul points out that the members of the church are the children of Abraham. Do you consider that the Jews who came through Abraham's loins, will be in the tribulation, so why not the gentiles then, for the text clearly says we are Abraham's seed. Here are some verses:

⁶ Even as Abraham believed God, and it was accounted to him for righteousness.⁷ And if ye be Christ's, then are ye Abraham's seed, and heirs according to the promise

14 That the blessing of Abraham might come on the Gentiles through Jesus Christ; that we might receive the promise of the Spirit through faith.

29 Know ye therefore that they which are of faith, the same are the children of Abraham. <u>Gal. 3.</u>

These are gentile Christians of Galatia that Paul was speaking to. Salvation comes through faith in Jesus Christ, and that by virtue of HIS death, burial and resurrection. Believers in Christ therefore become the children of Abraham by virtue of their faith in Christ, and by being Christ's, they become Abraham's children also, though not by blood. This is a mystical thing done by God. For the blessing of Abraham cometh on all believers through Jesus Christ, to receive the promise of the Spirit by faith. For Abraham believed God, and it was accounted unto him for righteousness. So if the Jews who are by birth related to Abraham through the lineage according to their blood, go through the tribulation, why not the gentile believers who are also Abrahams? We all belong to Christ, both Jews and Gentiles. We all will face the tribulation, yes, I tell you. There is no difference between the Jew and the Gentile in this regard, for we are both one in Christ's.

Secondly, since salvation came through the Jews, although as a nation they rejected Christ, we should not boast over them. Consider Romans 11. Israel is the root, and we the Gentiles are grafted in as wild olive branches unto the root, to join with them (Israel/the natural branches). The Gentiles therefore partake of the fatness of the olive tree with the Jews, why then will we not partake of the tribulation (leanness) of the tree that will occur. I tell you, we are as much a part of Israel as they are of us (the church). We are now the Israel of God, for we are both children of Abraham according to promise, and yes will therefore suffer tribulation at the appointed time. Tell me therefore, how the tree (representing the root/Israel) with branches on it, some grafted in as it were (rep. the gentiles/church), be in tribulation, and the root/tree be separated from its branches. Some of the branches remain that of the original/natural tree, but some wild/unnatural branches are grafted in. I tell you, it's one total tree, root, trunk and all branches together that will suffer, not one branch will be excluded. The exception being that the Lord will protect or shelter some of HIS people from the antichrist's hands at various safe places (example, in the wilderness), during this period of tribulation. It is a boast to suggest that the church will escape the tribulation, but Israel alone will suffer. That is why Jesus said, **"And except those days should be shortened, there should no flesh be saved: but for the elect's sake those days shall be shortened."** The word shortened means according to H. Stern, in the Jewish New Testament, 'limited'. I prefer this word for that is exactly what God does, limit the days to 1260, or 3 ½ yrs, and notice, it's **FOR THE ELECT'S SAKE.** Observe the text:

And if some of the branches be broken off, and thou, being a wild olive tree, wert grafted in among them, and with them partakest of the root and fatness of the olive tree; [18] Boast not against the branches. But if thou boast, thou bearest not the root, but the root thee.

[24] For if thou wert cut out of the olive tree which is wild by nature, and wert grafted contrary to nature into a good olive tree: how much more shall these, which be the natural branches, be grafted into their own olive tree? Rom. 11.

So we will suffer together, and Paul is telling us that the Jews will be grafted back into their own olive tree in time to come. Paul goes on to state in 2 Thess..: **" Seeing it is a righteous thing with God to recompense tribulation to them that trouble you". 2 Thess. 1:6-10.** This text is definitely speaking of the rapture and of Armageddon. So for the tribulation that we will suffer, the antichrist and all his followers will suffer vengeance at the Lord's hand on that day, yes, they will get a recompense of tribulation. Paul claimed the title of the "Apostle to the Gentiles", and this was a Gentile congregation that he had founded. Yet here was Paul telling them that they must suffer tribulation, and he associates their deliverance at the revealing of the Lord Jesus from heaven with HIS mighty angels at the rapture. Yes, this is the rapture and he then states that all who know not God and who disobey HIS gospel will be destroyed, everlastingly.

Third and last bit of dessert, here's Paul pointing out to the Gentiles of Ephesus, that through Christ we are now one. For before, scripture said we were classed as dogs and sorcerers, but according to Paul, we are now fellow-citizens with those who were considered holy (the circumcision/Jews/saints). But now we can lay claim to all the blessings by faith (circumcision/Jewry/sainthood), for the real Jew is one inwardly, and true circumcision is of the heart, spiritual not literal, and whose praise is not of men but of God. Recall also that Paul was an Hebrew, was an Israelite and was of the seed of Abraham. How quickly do we forget that the early Church suffered tribulation by way of persecutions, especially at the hands of the Roman Empire. Between A.D 30-A.D 311, about 12 of the 54 Emperors who ruled the Roman Empire, had Christians persecuted, according to Christianhistory.org.. Christians were sawn asunder, burnt at the stake, flogged publicly, imprisoned and stoned to death, becoming martyrs for their faith in Jesus Christ. Paul spoke of his experience in 2 Cor. 11, an experience that many more Christians suffered.

What makes us so special to avoid tribulation that the early Church suffered so badly, which we in modern times have not, for the most part. I tell you, yes, we all will go through the tribulation at the hands of the antichrist, you can bet on it. Apostle John was exiled to the Aegean island of Patmos in Asia Minor, in A.D 95 by Emperor Domitian, for his faith. That is tribulation my friend. Emperors such as Nero (54-68 A.D.), Domitian (81-96 A.D.), Trajan (98-117 A.D.), Marcus Aurelius (161-180 A.D.), Septimius Severus (193-211 A.D.), and Diocletian (284-305 A.D.) all directly and indirectly caused the persecution and death of many Christians during their various reigns. If it happened then, what will stop it from occurring at the

70th Week, and that to a greater degree moreso. What makes us more special than the Apostles and other believers who endured tremendous pain and sacrifice to see the gospel's proclamation and its increased reach to people. It was so devastating to these Christians back then, that they thought the 2nd coming of the Lord would have occurred from then. You had better think on these things. I will close here with Paul's letter to the Ephesians, showing the oneness of God's people See the text below:

[19] Now therefore ye are no more strangers and foreigners, but fellowcitizens with the saints, and of the household of God;

[20] And are built upon the foundation of the apostles and prophets, Jesus Christ himself being the chief corner stone; [21] In whom <u>all the building</u> fitly framed together groweth unto an holy temple in the Lord: Eph. 2:19-21.

I could draw more scriptures, but for what reason. We will all suffer tribulation, Israel and the Church, but the Church which includes Jews, will be raptured and the remnant of the Jews that are saved out of Israel, will inhabit Jerusalem in the Millennium. If you are yet unconvinced, God help you. I have said enough on the rapture, and must out of necessity move to my next topic which as I have said before, is intertwined with the rapture.

2 The Antichrist

In all of scripture, there are several characters that make up the total body of written work as it relates to the world empires and the time of the end. One such character is the man called the antichrist, who takes up a significant part of any end-times discussion. Rightly so too, for this man will be the opposite of Christ, and will come to dominate earth for a short period of time. There are several writers in the Bible who spoke about him, so I too must talk about him here. I will start by telling you that the antichrist is called by several different names by the various writers of the Bible, and I will examine them all, in a particular order. This, so as to build a sort of history on the figure, more like a pre-history, as he is not yet on the scene at the time of the writing of this book. It is most fascinating, that God writes history before it happens, humans can only record history after the fact.

In studying the antichrist, I began in Daniel, mainly due to a vision I had of him, revealed to me by the Lord Jesus way back in the late 1990s. This vision made me realize that he is not a current (2014-time of writing) world leader of a nation. He was expressly shown to me by the Lord, his total being, arriving on the world stage after a major war, so I am quite sure of this. For there to be a proper understanding of this man, one needs to begin in Daniel to get an understanding of the various world Empires as revealed to him by God. I had read before that many in Christianity view the antichrist as arising in Europe out of the Roman Empire, which they predicted would rise again. This belief came from a reading of **Dan. 9:27**, which said that **"and the people of the prince that shall come shall destroy the city and the sanctuary;"** They believed that this people of the prince (the antichrist) referred to the Roman soldiers who destroyed the city of Jerusalem and the Temple in AD 70. Historians are divided in their belief on this matter. Some say that it was (1) Roman (European) soldiers that destroyed Jerusalem and the Temple, while others point out that (2) the soldiers were Assyrian soldiers under the control of the Roman legion commanders, who were sent to destroy the city and Temple. Consequently, those of the 1st belief, think the Roman Empire will have a revival, and thus the antichrist will arise in Europe as that is where that Empire originated from (Rome) and expanded outwards. I have a very investigative mind and I decided to search the Bible to prove the truth to this theory bearing in mind that I had had a vision of the antichrist. I began this study in 2009, and within a year, I knew that it was incorrect, or put another way, the theory could not hold up as they believed. Without putting too much emphasis on this verse, I will use other texts to show the origins and abode of the antichrist.

Daniel had a vision of the various Empires which would rule the world until Christ came to defeat the last end time kingdom to be ruled by the antichrist. The vision was revealed to Daniel by the Lord God Himself. Let's see what Daniel had to say with regards to the kingdoms. I'll begin at Dan. 7:2, as this background information is crucial for overall understanding of the progressive development of the kingdoms to that of the antichrist. Here goes:

[2] **Daniel spake and said, I saw in my vision by night, and, behold, the four winds of the heaven strove upon the great sea. [3] And four great beasts came up from the sea, diverse one from another. [4] The first was like a lion, and had eagle's wings: I beheld till the wings thereof were plucked, and it was lifted up from the earth, and made stand upon the feet as a man, and a man's heart was given to it. [5] And behold another beast, a second, like to a bear, and it raised up itself on one side,**

and it had three ribs in the mouth of it between the teeth of it: and they said thus unto it, Arise, devour much flesh. [6] After this I beheld, and lo another, like a leopard, which had upon the back of it four wings of a fowl; the beast had also four heads; and dominion was given to it.

[7] After this I saw in the night visions, and behold a fourth beast, dreadful and terrible, and strong exceedingly; and it had great iron teeth: it devoured and brake in pieces, and stamped the residue with the feet of it: and it was diverse from all the beasts that were before it; and it had ten horns. [8] I considered the horns, and, behold, there came up among them another little horn, before whom there were three of the first horns plucked up by the roots: and, behold, in this horn were eyes like the eyes of man, and a mouth speaking great things..........

[17] These great beasts, which are four, are four kings, which shall arise out of the earth. [18] But the saints of the most High shall take the kingdom, and possess the kingdom for ever, even for ever and ever. [19] Then I would know the truth of the fourth beast, which was diverse [different] from all the others, exceeding dreadful, whose teeth were of iron, and his nails of brass; which devoured, brake in pieces, and stamped the residue with his feet; [20] And of the ten horns that were in his head, and of the other which came up, and before whom three fell; even of that horn that had eyes, and a mouth that spake very great things, whose look was more stout than his fellows.

[21] I beheld, and the same horn made war with the saints, and prevailed against them; [22] Until the Ancient of days came, and judgment was given to the saints of the most High; and the time came that the saints possessed the kingdom. [23] Thus he said, The fourth beast shall be the fourth kingdom upon earth, which shall be diverse from all kingdoms, and shall devour the whole earth, and shall tread it down, and break it in pieces. [24] And the ten horns out of this kingdom are ten kings that shall arise: and another shall rise after them; and he shall be diverse from the first, and he shall subdue three kings. [25] And he shall speak great words against the most High, and shall wear out the saints of the most High, and think to change times and laws: and they shall be given into his hand until a time and times and the dividing of time. [3 ½ yrs/1260 days]. [26] But the judgment shall sit, and they shall take away his dominion, to consume and to destroy it unto the end. Dan. 7.

History proves that Daniel was quite right, and quite so, after all he was shown the vision by God, who cannot lie. Accordingly, here's what Daniel described of the four beasts which he saw:

1) Lion with eagles wings
2) Bear with 3 ribs in mouth
3) Leopard with 4 wings, 4 heads
4) Fourth beast –had great iron teeth, and then ten horns.

The 4th beast had ten horns among whom another **little horn** came up. This new horn uprooted three of the original ten. This is Daniel's first mention of the antichrist figure (the little horn) though he is not called the antichrist by him.

What Daniel saw from his vision (1- 4), were the Empires which later came to rule the world. History records them as follows:

1) Babylonian Empire
2) Medo-Persian Empire
3) Grecian Empire
4) Roman Empire.

The descriptions of the beasts as given by Daniel fitted perfectly the actual beginnings, conquering of lands and eventual defeat of each beast by the following beast kingdom. It took me several years of studying to realize that the fourth beast above (Roman Empire) would be followed by two more Empires with the final being the one to produce the antichrist. If you read **Dan. 7** alone, you may become confused as I was, for the fourth beast (the Roman Empire), "seemed" to have the little horn which would become the antichrist (v 7e, 8, 20, 23-26), although another Empire did arise after the Roman Empire. However a careful reading of other Daniel passages and then comparing them with Revelation, opened my understanding and banished my confusion.

Each of these Empires had more than one King during their time of supremacy, but always had at least one notable King. For example, the reign of the Babylonian Empire began with Nebuchadnezzar, just as he had seen of the image in his dream. It was Daniel alone who was able to both describe what the King had dreamt as well as to explain the dream to the king. This is discussed in Daniel chap. 2. Here it is:

[31] **Thou, O king, sawest, and behold a great image. This great image, whose brightness was excellent, stood before thee; and the form thereof was terrible.** [32] **This image's head was of fine gold, his breast and his arms of silver, his belly and his thighs of brass,** [33] **His legs of iron, his feet part of iron and part of clay.**

[34] **Thou sawest till that a stone was cut out without hands, which smote the image upon his feet that were of iron and clay, and brake them to pieces.** [35] **Then was the iron, the clay, the brass, the silver, and the gold, broken to pieces together, and became like the chaff of the summer threshingfloors; and the wind carried them away, that no place was found for them: and the stone that smote the image became a great mountain, and filled the whole earth.**

[41] **And whereas thou sawest the feet and toes, part of potters' clay, and part of iron, the kingdom shall be divided;**

38 b. Thou art this head of gold. <u>Dan. 2.</u>

This was actually Daniel's first recorded vision as it appeared in chapter 2. Yes, for God revealed to him what Nebuchadnezzar had dreamt, what Nebuchadnezzar's astrologers,_magicians, sorcerers and the Chaldeans could not reveal to him. As I've said before, each Empire had at least one notable King. Nebuchadnezzar was the most notable King of the Babylonian Empire. Alexander the Great was the most notable leader of the Grecian Empire. It is from **Dan. 2** that had the dream of the image that showed a ten toes mixture of iron and clay, that I drew my first comparison to **Dan. 7:7** dream of the 4th beast with ten horns. Notice though that Dan. 7 says, **";and it had ten horns."** But notice this is after a semi-colon. Now I have come to realize that colons, semi-colons and full stops in the Bible must be read carefully, for it could mean that a big time span has taken place. Yes in many cases, a year, years, even hundreds of years may pass after these signs before the next verse continues. Therefore one should never read the Bible quickly especially when studying prophecy, for you may miss the whole story if you don't see the time gap. Such a time gap occurs here, for the 4th beast of Dan. 7 (the Roman Empire), did not of itself produce the antichrist then. In fact, even though the 4th beast has the ten horns from which comes up another little horn, this has not occurred yet, but will at the time of the end (the 70th Week). The ten horns (similar to the ten toes of chap. 2) is actually another Empire that will arise after the Roman Empire. Notice that v. 6 of chap. 7 describes the **3rd beast - a leopard**- with four heads. This described the speed of Alexander the Great's, conquest of the Medo-Persia Empire. He later died young (age 32) and his kingdom was then divided up among his four generals. These generals, namely, Ptolemy, Seleucis, Cassander and Lysimachus took control over four regions of the Empire. Seleucis controlled Syria and Babylonia region, along with Palestine eventually. This major land mass is north of Israel while on the other hand, Ptolemy assumed control over the lands south of Israel, Egypt and its environs.

The Seleucids fought several wars with the Ptolemys, and Israel was caught right in the middle of these wars. The Seleucids eventually controlled Jerusalem; their King became known as the King of the North, being north of Israel, with his headquarters being in Syria. The Ptolemys became known as the King of the South (Egypt), see Dan. 11:1-20 for excerpts of some of the wars between these Kings. From v. 21-45, it speaks of the antichrist's rise to power and eventual 3 ½ yrs reign until his destruction by God. In these verses you see the antichrist being called a vile person and then also as the King of the North, **thus revealing from which of the four general's region he would arise – that of SELEUCIS (see map of Seleucid region).** Remember that from among the ten horns came up another little horn which subdued 3 of the original horns. This new horn would also speak against the most High, attack the saints (3 ½ yrs?) and think to change times and laws (**Dan. 7**). Now Daniel chapter 8 confirms that this 'little horn' that comes up among the ten (chap. 7), is the same as that horn which comes up, after the great horn (Alexander the Great) was broken, and four notable ones came up (the four generals) toward the four winds of heaven. Observe keenly, the comparison made here of the little horn between chaps. 7 & 8. Notice that in **chap. 8:9,** "And out of one of them [one of the four] came forth a little horn", which is similar to **Dan.7:8,** "and, behold, there came up among them [among the ten] another little horn." This horn does the same things – he attacks the saints and fight against God, thus it is the same horn. Notice then more information about the little horn is given, it now possesses human personality and is identified as a "he". This is the antichrist. This "he" also makes the **transgression of desolation** [on Temple Mount]. **"The daily sacrifice was taken away, it cast down the truth to the ground, through his policy also he shall cause craft to prosper in his hand; and he shall magnify himself in his heart, and by peace shall destroy many."** This is the one and only man of sin/lawlessness as stated by Paul in 2 Thessalonian, the son of perdition, the antichrist. Here is the Daniel 8 text:

Then I lifted up mine eyes, and saw, and, behold, there stood before the river a ram which had two horns: and the two horns were high; but one was higher than the other, and the higher came up last.

[4] I saw the ram pushing westward, and northward, and southward; so that no beasts might stand before him, neither was there any that could deliver out of his hand; but he did according to his will, and became great. [5] And as I was considering, behold, an he goat came from the west on the face of the whole earth, and touched not the ground: and the goat had a notable horn between his eyes. [6] And he came to the ram that had two horns, which I had seen standing before the river, and ran unto him in the fury of his power.

[7] And I saw him come close unto the ram, and he was moved with choler against him, and smote the ram, and brake his two horns: and there was no power in the ram to stand before him, but he cast him down to the ground, and stamped upon him: and there was none that could deliver the ram out of his hand. [8] Therefore

the he goat waxed very great: and when he was strong, the great horn was broken; and for it came up four notable ones toward the four winds of heaven. [9] And out of one of them came forth a little horn, which waxed exceeding great, toward the south, and toward the east, and toward the pleasant land.

[10] And it waxed great, even to the host of heaven; and it cast down some of the host and of the stars to the ground, and stamped upon them. [11] Yea, he magnified himself even to the prince of the host, and by him the daily sacrifice was taken away, and the place of the sanctuary was cast down. [12] And an host was given him against the daily sacrifice by reason of transgression, and it cast down the truth to the ground; and it practised, and prospered. [13] Then I heard one saint speaking, and another saint said unto that certain saint which spake, How long shall be the vision concerning the daily sacrifice, and the transgression of desolation, to give both the sanctuary and the host to be trodden under foot? [14] And he said unto me, Unto two thousand and three hundred days; then shall the sanctuary be cleansed. [15] And it came to pass, when I, even I Daniel, had seen the vision, and sought for the meaning, then, behold, there stood before me as the appearance of a man.

[16] And I heard a man's voice between the banks of Ulai, which called, and said, Gabriel, make this man to understand the vision. [17] So he came near where I stood: and when he came, I was afraid, and fell upon my face: but he said unto me, Understand, O son of man: for at the time of the end shall be the vision. [18] Now as he was speaking with me, I was in a deep sleep on my face toward the ground: but he touched me, and set me upright. [19] And he said, Behold, I will make thee know what shall be in the last end of the indignation: for at the time appointed the end shall be.

[20] The ram which thou sawest having two horns are the kings of Media and Persia. [21] And the rough goat is the king of Grecia: and the great horn that is between his eyes is the first king. [22] Now that being broken, whereas four stood up for it, four kingdoms shall stand up out of the nation, but not in his power. [23] And in the latter time of their kingdom, when the transgressors are come to the full, a king of fierce countenance, and understanding dark sentences, shall stand up. [24] And his power shall be mighty, but not by his own power: and he shall destroy wonderfully, and shall prosper, and practise, and shall destroy the mighty and the holy people.

[25] And through his policy also he shall cause craft to prosper in his hand; and he shall magnify himself in his heart, and by peace shall destroy many: he shall also stand up against the Prince of princes; but he shall be broken without

hand. [26] And the vision of the evening and the morning which was told is true: wherefore shut thou up the vision; for it shall be for many days. [27] And I Daniel fainted, and was sick certain days; afterward I rose up, and did the king's business; and I was astonished at the vision, but none understood it. Dan. 8

So then it is quite apparent that the beast of **Daniel 7**, (the 4th which is the Roman Empire) that seemingly produces the little horn –the antichrist- is intricately linked with the beast of **Daniel 8**. For in **Daniel 8**, the little horn – the antichrist- is seen coming from one of the four kingdoms that arises after the fall of Alexander the Great. These four kingdoms arose still within the reign of the Grecian Empire, albeit the latter part, so it's not really the 4th beast, but the 3rd beast that produces the little horn. In other words, it is the Grecian Empire that produces the little horn in the end of its kingdom, when the transgressors are come to the full, according to this vision of Daniel. However, notice that the Grecian Empire is not now in view, as the Roman Empire actually succeeded it, which was then itself succeeded by the Ottoman Islamic Empire. So let there be no confusion between the various dreams, God just skillfully shows the place/region that the antichrist will come from, from the Grecian's 'one of the four', and from the "Roman" end time ten horns. But IT'S NOT REALLY THE ROMAN, that has the ten horns, but the Ottoman Islamic Empire, which succeeded the Roman Empire. Please observe carefully!!! Observe v7 of chap. 7 very carefully, especially, from " : and it was diverse..." Today we are in a time gap between the 7th and the 8th Empire, interestingly we are in a time gap between the 69th and 70th Week. The Apostle John in Rev. 17, stated that the 8th beast is of the [7th] [or from the 7th], and goeth into perdition [destruction]. Therefore, since the 4th beast of Daniel is the Roman Empire, which is succeeded by the Ottoman Islamic Empire from which the little horn comes up amongst the ten horns; and since the 3rd beast (Grecian Empire) that the little horn comes out of, from among the four latter kingdoms of its reign, which is the Seleucid; and now in Rev. 17, he is the 8th from the 7th, then there must be a common thread or a bridge that links these Empires, for they are all shown to produce the antichrist. Notice John calls it the 7th of 8th, why? **The answer – it must be the bloodline or put another way, it is the SAME heritage, i.e., the same blood related people**. Just as the Jews trace their heritage back to Abraham, so too will the antichrist's heritage be traceable back to those who ruled the Seleucid kingdom, for they were before the Roman Empire, 3 comes before 4, right? **Also, it is the Ottoman Islamic Empire that will be revived in the future**.

Therefore, to go back to the people of the prince, I subscribe to the belief that it was Assyrian soldiers controlled by Roman commanders who destroyed Jerusalem, **this is the people of the prince that shall come**. For it is clear that the little horn comes from Middle Eastern heritage, as the Grecian and Ottoman Islamic Empires were. The Assyrians ARE certainly of Middle Eastern heritage, not European. As it relates to the Seleucids, Grecian and Ottoman Empires, only bloodline could cross or continue through so many generations of people, through several centuries, make no mistake about it. For they all will have a hand or a relationship in bringing forth the little horn, or the antichrist. John in Revelation 13, laid out a picture of the beast as "like unto a leopard [Grecian], and his feet were as the feet of a bear [Medo-Persia], and his mouth as the mouth of a lion [Babylon]: and the dragon gave him his power, and his seat, and great authority." Clearly this is a composite beast which corresponds to that of Dan. 7 & 8, for the antichrist comes out of them. It tells me that the antichrist will have all the characteristics of these Empires within him, or certainly within the reign of his Empire until God destroys him (the stone that strikes the statue's feet in Dan. 2). He will possess riches, he will be strong (for a while), he will crush his enemies (for a while), his attacks and conquests will be swift, and he will be feared and worshipped by many.

Please peruse the following image replica of Daniel 2, and some related maps of the various world Empires as seen by Daniel and John. I have set them out in the order of the rise of the Empires as they succeeded each other. On the image, the Roman Empire is represented by the two legs of iron, but notice that afterwards there are two feet of a mixture of iron and clay. This is really the Ottoman Islamic Empire, which followed after. This Empire had a mixture of Muslim Arabs and Roman peoples, for it covered part of Europe – a carry-over from the past era. The antichrist comes out of the area formerly occupied by the Seleucids, which is so named after one of the four generals that followed the fall of Alexander the Great. **This area (see Grecian & Seleucid maps) covers lands that are now occupied by countries such as Syria, Lebanon, Israel, Iraq, Iran, Turkey and Jordan – seven nations of the Middle East today.** Interestingly, these same regions were once controlled by all the Empires from the Assyrian, Babylonian, Medo-Persian, Grecian, Roman and Ottoman time periods. When you look at the other names that the antichrist is called by, there is no doubt where he will rise and have his center of operations – the Middle East. How do prophecy teachers get him rising in Europe – all because of the one text in Daniel 9:27 - "the people of the prince that shall come."

The Empires covered more lands but I am highlighting these countries, as here is where the major concerns/activities will come from. These nations or lands, along with Egypt, have always been central to almost all Bible prophecies and happenings from ancient of days. Indeed, today (2015) these countries are in turmoil with some suffering from Arab spring wars (Egypt), or civil wars (Iraq & Syria), or infighting and power struggles between Muslims of Sunni or Shiite beliefs. Now there is a new player on the field since 2014, called ISIS – Islamic State of Iraq and Syria, or ISIL – Islamic State of Iraq and the Levant. They have added to the various Al-qaeda and Taliban groups that were before ISIS. Thousands of lives have been lost and there seems no end to the tide of bloodletting which include shootings and suicide bombings among other types of killings. **So look for the antichrist to rise in the Middle East and nowhere else.** I predict that he will then conquer the rest of the Middle East, Europe, perhaps Asia and then the west as in the Americas and Caribbean, for he will rule the world, but his main center of operations will always be the Middle East.

The antichrist will not necessarily be everywhere at the same time, whilst ruling the world. Only the ONE and only Almighty God reserves that privilege, for HE alone is omnipresent, omnipotent and omniscient. The President of the United States, or any country for that matter, cannot be everywhere in the country at the same time, but he rules nonetheless. How does he do this? By having or appointing other sub-leaders such as state governors, with their own state legislatures. The former World Empires all had one leader at a time but then had other secondary leaders in the outlying provinces or regions, that had immediate control over local matters but who had to report to the leader-Emperor. For example, the Roman Emperor, Nero, had as governor of the Province of Judaea, Marcus Antonius Felix (52-60 A.D.). This was during the time of the Apostle Paul when he came before the governor for trial (Acts 24). The antichrist himself hints at this same scenario in **Isa. 10:8, For he saith, Are not my princes altogether kings?** Thus he will set up sub-commanders in various countries to rule for him, but will always be a dictator at heart, for he eventually posits himself as God, in the Temple.

See combined, comparative descriptive chart of all the Empires on the next several pages.

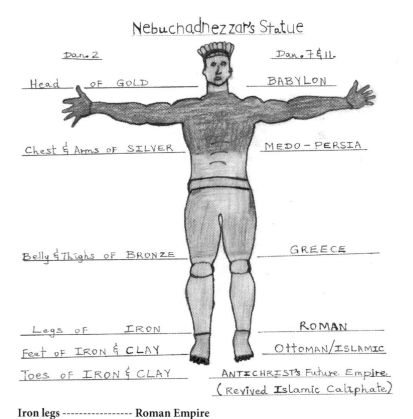

Nebuchadnezzar's Statue

Dan. 2		Dan. 7 & 11.
Head of GOLD		BABYLON
Chest & Arms of SILVER		MEDO – PERSIA
Belly & Thighs of BRONZE		GREECE
Legs of IRON		ROMAN
Feet of IRON & CLAY		Ottoman/ISLAMIC
Toes of IRON & CLAY		ANTICHRIST's Future Empire (Revived Islamic Caliphate)

Iron legs ----------------- Roman Empire
Iron & clay feet --------- Ottoman Empire
Iron & clay ten toes ---- Antichrist's future Empire (Revived Islamic Caliphate)

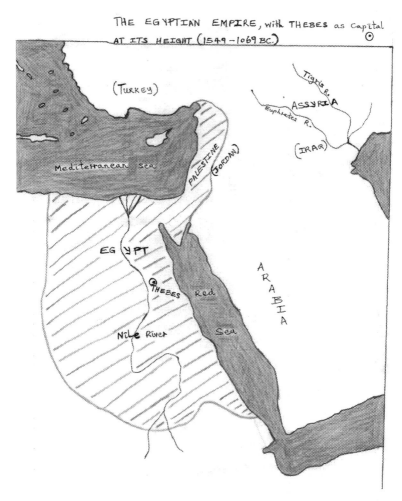

THE EGYPTIAN EMPIRE, with THEBES as Capital AT ITS HEIGHT (1549 - 1069 BC.)

(TURKEY)

Tigris R.

ASSYRIA

Euphrates R.

(IRAQ)

Mediterranean sea

PALESTINE

(JORDAN)

EGYPT

THEBES

Red

Nile River

Sea

A R A B I A

<u>The Egyptian Empire</u>

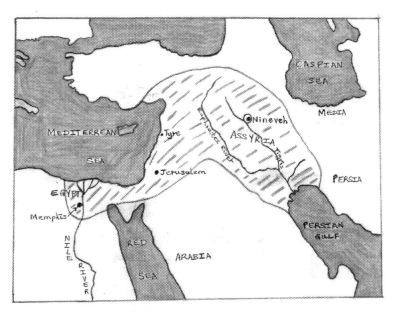

THE ASSYRIAN EMPIRE
Est. boundary ▬
⊙ Capital : Nineveh

<u>The Assyrian Empire</u>

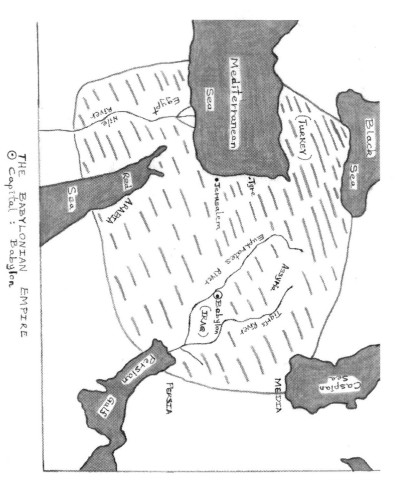

The Babylonian Empire

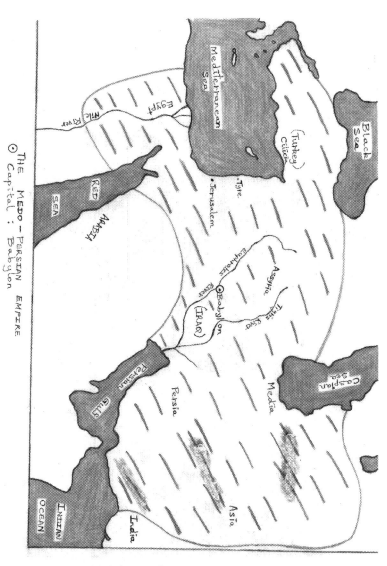

The Medo-Persian Empire

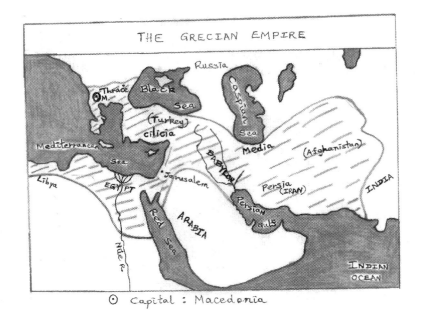

<u>The Grecian Empire – 323 BC</u>

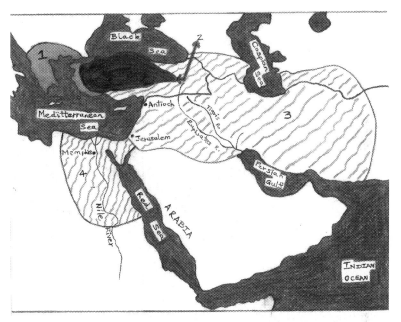

The four notable kingdoms after Alexander's death

The four notable kingdoms that formed after Alexander the Great died. They were formed by four of his generals.

1) Cassander – Macedonia and Greece
2) Lysimachus -- Thrace and Bythinia
3) Seleucis -- Syria and Babylonia
4) Ptolemy – Egypt, Palestine, Arabia

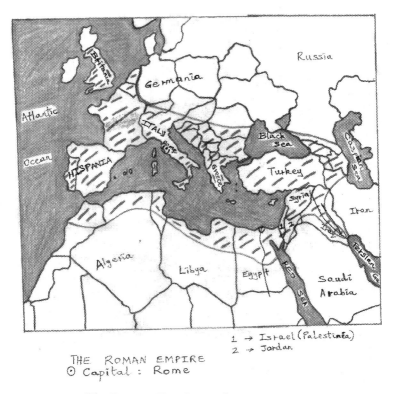

1 → Israel (Palestina)
2 → Jordan

THE ROMAN EMPIRE
⊙ Capital : Rome

The Roman Empire at about 116> A.D.

The Ottomans overthrew the eastern leg of the Roman Empire (Byzantine) with the 1453 conquest of Constantinople (present-day Istanbul) by Mehmud the Conqueror. The Ottomans eventually conquered the Roman Empire.

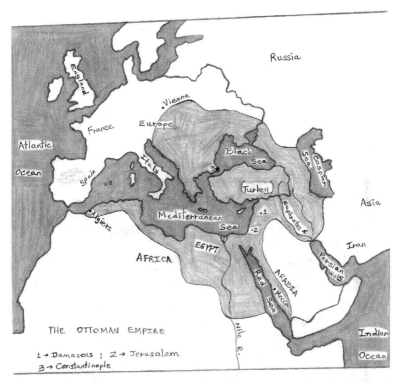

THE OTTOMAN EMPIRE

1 → Damascus ; 2 → Jerusalem
3 → Constantinople

The Ottoman Islamic Empire: Greek and Arab nationalism, led to revolts against the Ottoman Empire. They were supported by European nationalism in these revolts, with Turkey being first declared independent of the Empire. This eventually led to World War one, where In WWI (1914-1918), the Ottomans sided with the Germans, and Hungarians - Austrians against Russia, France, and Britain. The Ottomans and its allies lost to those of the British, who then divided up the Arab world between Britain and France. Arbitrary lines were drawn on the map to divide up the Arab world into new states called Transjordan, Syria, Iraq, Lebanon, and Palestine. Zionist Jews were encouraged to settle in Palestine, creating a new Jewish state – Israel. Egypt continued under British domination to become its own nation, separate from the rest of the Arab world. What had once been the great Ottoman Empire was no more, it was replaced by numerous competing and disunited nationalistic states. See next map.

Flag of the Ottoman Empire (1844-1923)

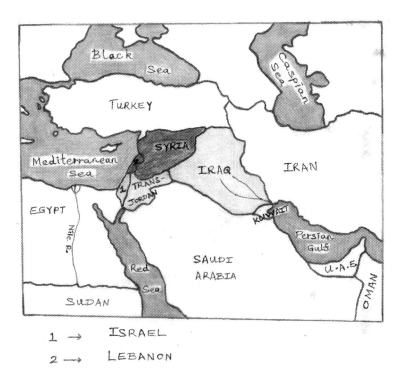

1 → ISRAEL

2 → LEBANON

The Sykes-Picot Agreement of 1916 divided up the Ottoman Empire among the British and the French. This led to a period of further wars and consolidation which eventually saw some of these countries gaining independence. Countries such as Turkey (1923), Syria (1944), Jordan (1946), Iraq (1947), Egypt (1947), and Israel (1948) were established as independent nations. Iran was already an independent nation and had their own Parliament established from as far back as 1906. It was called Persia until around 1935.

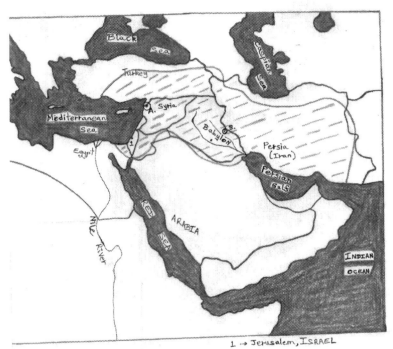

1 → Jerusalem, ISRAEL

THE SELEUCID KINGDOM
⊙ Capital (S.)Seleucia and then Antioch (A.)

Map of the Seleucid Empire - Antiochus IV
(175-164 BC), was the 8th ruler of the Seleucid Empire.

COMPARING DANIEL'S & JOHN'S VISIONS OF THE EMPIRES

Before Daniel, there were two Empires, the Egyptian Empire and the Assyrian Empire. So in fact the Empires should rightly look like this:

EMPIRE	DANIEL 2	DANIEL 7	DANIEL 8	DANIEL 11	REVELATION 13 & 17
EGYPTIAN 1560-1080 B.C. ?	-------	--------	-------	--------	**Rev. 17:10**
ASSYRIAN 1250-612 B.C. ?	-------	--------	-------	--------	**Rev. 17:10**
BABYLONIAN 606-536 B.C. ?	Head of Gold **vs. 32, 38**	Lion - **vs. 4,17** **(Jer. 4:7,13)**	------	------	Mouth of the Lion (1 head) **Rev.13: 2**
MEDO – PERSIA 539-331 B.C. ?	Chest of Silver **vs. 32, 39**	Bear (1 side higher) **vs. 5, 17**	Ram w/ 2 horns (1 higher) **vs. 3, 20**	Kings of Persia **vs. 1-3**	Feet of the Bear (1 head) **Rev.13: 2**
GRECIAN (Alexander the Great) 332-146 B.C. ?	Belly of Brass **vs. 32, 39**	Leopard w/ 4 heads 4 wings ** **vs. 6, 17**	He-Goat w/ 4 successors ** **vs. 5, 21-22**	Mighty King **vs. 3-4**	Body of the Leopard (4 heads) ** **Rev.13: 2**
ROMAN Founded 753 B.C., Expanded 241 B.C. - 27 B.C.- 476 A.D.	Legs of Iron **vs. 33, 40**	4th Diverse Beast Iron Teeth **vs. 7, 17**	------	Crucifixion of Christ, Fall of Jerusalem 70 A.D. **v. 22**	Empire of John's time. 'Five are fallen and **one is'** **Rev.17:10**
OTTOMAN (Muslim) 1299-1923 A.D.	Feet of iron & clay **v 33**	Feet stamped residue, **v 7**	-------	--------	7th **Head** (wounded) **Rev. 13: 3** Beast continue for a short space, **Rev.17:10**
ANTICHRIST (Muslim) near future, last 3 ½ yrs- Armageddon	Toes (10) of iron & clay **v 41**	Ten horns, then another little horn ** **vs 7-8**	Fierce countenance King ** **v 23**	Vile person, v 21. King of the North, **v 40.**	8th beast from the 7th And goeth into perdition, 10 horns; **10 toes of Dan.2** **Rev.17:11-12**

** **The King of fierce countenance (little horn/antichrist) comes from one of this four or ten.**

1) Egyptian Empire
2) Assyrian Empire
3) Babylonian Empire
4) Medo-Persian Empire
5) Grecian Empire
6) Roman Empire
7) Ottoman Empire
8) **Antichrist Empire** – the little horn that comes out of one of the four kingdoms (Seleucid) that Alexander the Great's, Grecian Empire was divided into, after his fall. It must be pointed out though that this Antichrist Empire has not occurred as yet, for the Roman Empire actually succeeded the Grecian Empire, and the Ottoman Empire followed the Roman. Thus, it's the 8th head (Antichrist/Muslim Empire) which is of the 7th head (Ottoman Muslim Empire).

So the antichrist is the 8th head or empire which will rule the world, and comes out of the 7th (Ottoman Empire). To go back to the question asked before, why does John say the 8th of the 7th, when Daniel saw four Empires. Well the answer lies in the fact that God revealed to Daniel the four Empires from his time, which were the Babylonian, Medo-Persian, Grecian and Roman Empires. However, there were two other Empires before Daniel's time which Daniel, wise as he was, must have known about. These were first, the Egyptian Empire and next in line, the Assyrian Empire. On the other hand, to John was revealed the Roman Empire the 6th; the one that was "is") and the one to come, the Ottoman Empire, (the 7th), which would be followed by the 8th, the Antichrist Empire for the last 3 ½ years. Daniel was among the Jews who were taken captive from Judah in Israel by King Nebuchadnezzar of Babylon in approximately 604 B.C. (Dan.1). The prophet Jeremiah foretold this to last for 70 years, as God had foretold (Jer. 25), and Daniel himself lived and served in prominent positions in the governments of several Babylonian and Medo-Persian rulers, inclusive of Nebuchadnezzar, Belshazzar (Babylonian) and Darius and Cyrus (Medo-Persian). John in a similar vein, lived during the reign of the Roman Empire, which encompassed the birth, life, death and resurrection of Jesus Christ. John was the last of the Apostles to die, while he was on the Isle of Patmos.

So as shown in the maps, the Empires should really look like this in the table below:

1) Egyptian Empire ----------- before Daniel's time.
2) Assyrian Empire ------------ before Daniel's time.
3) Babylonian Empire --------- during Daniel's time – the 1st he envisioned.
4) Medo-Persian Empire ------ part of Daniel's time – the 2nd he envisioned.
5) Grecian Empire ------------- Daniel's 3rd Empire that he envisioned.

6) Roman Empire ------------- Daniel's 4th Empire that he
envisioned; John's 6th.

7) Ottoman Empire ----------- John's7th.

8) **Antichrist Empire** ---------- **John's 8th, which is of the 7th.**

See combined, comparative descriptive chart of all the Empires on the next several pages.

The Egyptian Empire went as far back as before the time of Joseph (Jacob's son), and after, who was sold into Egypt by his brothers. The Assyrian Empire succeeded the Egyptian Empire. Then Daniel came on the scene during the Babylonian Empire and was shown all the Empires – the two that were before him, he would have known about them either by reading or by revelation from God. He spoke of the 1st Empire (the Babylonian) which he described as the first of the four he visioned, however Babylon was actually the 3rd of eight Empires. Daniel only described four. However, he saw the feet of iron and clay, as well as the ten toes of the image which represents the final nations at the time of the end, from among whom the antichrist will come; he also saw the ten horns among whom came up another little horn, in another vision; he also saw that the antichrist would come from the specific region of the Seleucid Kingdom – a region that include countries today such as Turkey, Lebanon, Israel, Syria, Iraq, Iran and Jordan. Thus Daniel saw all the Empires.

Then God also showed the same Empires to John, though not in the same way, but in keeping with the principle explained earlier, John would also have known of them through reading or by the revelation of God. John lived during the Roman Empire. Here God shows another Bible principle, that of using more than one writer to explain the same visions, prophecies or doctrines. For John said, **"there are seven kings: five are fallen** [Egypt, Assyria, Babylon, Medo-Persia, & Grecia], **and one is** [Roman] **and the other is not yet come;** [Ottoman]. **Rev.17:10.** What a great God – as scripture says,"in the mouth of two or three witnesses, a thing is established."

Therefore, John knew what he was saying, in that, he knew there were then six Empires, with two to follow. In v.11, John rightly thus stated ....**even he is the eighth, and is of the seven**.....so John also saw the eight Empires although he described it differently. Upon close examination of the facts as described by both Daniel and John, it is VERY CLEAR that both are saying the SAME THING.

The antichrist therefore will come from the lineage of the Greek kings under the Grecian Empire, with links to the Roman and Ottoman Empires. It is therefore all these Empires which will be revived in the person of the antichrist, not just the Roman Empire as some believe. That is why John shows a composite beast in Rev. 13 and 17. The antichrist's conquests will be swift (like Grecia), his rule will be hard and harsh, iron-like (like Roman), and will be mixed (Arabs, Europeans, Asians) just like the Ottoman in terms of his people, both in leadership as well as followers. The bloodline of evil, dictatorial leadership, disrespect and antagonism towards God and God's people will be seen at its fullest extent during the reign of the man of sin. One only has to study the history of one of the progenitors, the famous Antiochus Epiphanes (of whom a bust is built), to begin to visualize the type of cruelty and contempt shown towards God and HIS people that will occur in the 3 ½ yrs reign of the antichrist. See the picture of the Seleucid Kingdom that Antiochus once ruled, as their eighth king. It is from this lineage that the antichrist will come, you can bet on it. Indeed several prophecy writers and many believers, and some Jews think that Dan. 11:21-45 was completely fulfilled by Antiochus. However, a careful reading of the said verses proves that though Antiochus may have fulfilled some aspect of the text, he is not the one being spoken of here.

This text (11:21-45), is talking about the time of the end and is definitely speaking of the antichrist. There are many verses that can be used to show it's not Antiochus but I will just choose one, v 31, **And arms shall stand on his part, and they shall pollute the sanctuary of strength, and shall <u>take away the daily sacrifice</u>, and they <u>shall place the</u>**

<u>abomination that maketh desolate</u>. This very verse was referred to by Jesus when HE was talking to his Disciples in Matt. 24, when in v.15, HE said, **¹⁵ When ye therefore shall see the <u>abomination of desolation</u>, spoken of by Daniel the prophet;"** Jesus said that the people in Judaea should flee. He was speaking of the end-time period of trouble that would occur especially in Israel, the time that Jeremiah called, **the time of Jacob's trouble.** So even if Antiochus fulfilled some aspect of v31, he is not the person being referred to. Jesus further stated that "immediately after the tribulation of those days", that there would be signs in the heavens and then would appear the sign of the son of man in heaven. This is the Lord Jesus' return for HIS elect, so it is clear that both Jesus and Daniel were referring to the same future man – the antichrist.

As history will have proclaimed, Antiochus was violently bitter against the Jews, and was determined to exterminate them and their religion. He did several terrible deeds to the Jews, inclusive of devastating Jerusalem in 168 BC. He defiled the Temple by offering a pig on its altar, then erected an altar to Jupiter, and prohibited the Jews from doing Temple worship. He also forbade the Jews from doing circumcision, and sold thousands of Jewish families into slavery. He destroyed all copies of Scripture that could be found, and slaughtered everyone discovered in possession of such copies, and resorted to all kinds of conceivable torture to force Jews to renounce their religion. The antichrist will do likewise, but at a far more terrifying degree and pace. I believe I read somewhere before, where a writer said that the antichrist will make Hitler, the Nazi, look like a choirboy. Just think of the over 6 million Jews and other people that died at the hands of Hitler's cruel regime in the 1930s-1940s, and multiply that perhaps fivefold or more, and you will begin to see the utter devastation that the antichrist will bring in his rise to power and in the second part of the Week (the last 3 ½ yrs), when he officially reigns. It is no wonder the Lord limits his time to just 3 ½ years/1260 days or 42 months, otherwise no flesh would be saved.

Therefore I believe the antichrist will be in the lineage of Antiochus who is a sort of forerunner to the antichrist. Perhaps if it were possible to do it, a bloodline trace of the antichrist could be done right back to Antiochus, and possibly back to some earlier evil men also. **It's the same bloodline.** When he brings forth the mandatory mark of the beast through the false prophet, it will be a very terrible time on earth, but the Lord will shield and protect HIS people during this time, though some must be killed by the sword (not literal sword, but may include that weapon among other types) as scripture stated. Here's an interesting thought, I believe the antichrist will not know he is destined to be the antichrist/the man of sin, until power and pride gets to his head, and he foolishly ascends to the Temple and declares himself as God. However he will be very wicked and cruel from the very beginning of his rise to power, but will manage to hide his murderous character through flattery, guile, trickery and deceit. Many will be tricked by these skill-sets, for by peace he shall destroy many. The aura of his power, though not of himself, will captivate many. He will be a boaster, and will accomplish many things that will seem great to the populace, but when he is taken over by the devil at the midway point of the seven years, the final 1260 days, then and only then, will his true colours be shown, and he will know then that he is the antichrist. No wonder he sets about slaughtering as many of God's people as he can as per Revelation 12:16-17. He will claim to be God, and may even perform some seemingly miraculous things, but he will come to his end at Armageddon, when the Lord shall destroy him with the brightness of HIS coming.

The antichrist will think that whatever he does is by his own doing and by the power of his god, when in fact it is the Lord God who sets him up to attack Israel, for there is no power, but of God. Ultimately the world will come under his sway, but man's rebellious nature of self-rule will be brought to an end at the battle of Armageddon. Is the antichrist found by other names in the Bible? You bet, there are several such names by which we find the antichrist scattered throughout several books of the Bible. It is by some of these names that I came to realize that the antichrist must rise in the Middle East. He must rise within the area covered by the former Seleucid Empire, said area almost mirroring that of the Grecian Empire. Again, observe what Daniel said and consider the present day nations noted above, that it is basically the same land area. Borders and names may have changed but it is the same region. A careful reading of the various texts that I will include here will leave the reader in no doubt whatsoever. The reader is here encouraged to read all the texts to get the full understanding of God's revelation of the antichrist long before the New Testament. I will give one or two verses and ask that you continue further reading as pointed out. Here are the names.

The Assyrian

[5] **O Assyrian**, the rod of mine anger, and the staff in their hand is mine indignation.

[24] Therefore thus saith the Lord GOD of hosts, O my people that dwellest in Zion, be not afraid of **the Assyrian**: **Isa.10:5&24.**

Further reading: Isa. 10:4-14, 24-26. In this text, you find God bringing the Assyrian [antichrist] against a hypocritical nation. Look at the map and see the region covered by the Assyrian Empire, namely Iraq, Jordan, Lebanon, Syria, parts of Iran and Turkey stretching to Egypt. **Its capital was Nineveh in Iraq.** So a future Assyrian King will rule again, in the person of the antichrist.

[25] That I will break **the Assyrian** in my land, and upon my mountains tread him under foot: then shall his yoke depart from off them, and his burden depart from off their shoulders. **Read Isa 14:24-27.**

See also Isa. 30:30-31; and Isa. 31:5, 8-9. Micah5:6.

King of Babylon, or Babylon and Chaldee/Chaldean

The burden of **Babylon**, which Isaiah the son of Amoz did see.

¹⁹ And **Babylon**, the glory of kingdoms, the beauty of **the Chaldees' excellency**, shall be as when God overthrew Sodom and Gomorrah. **Isa. 13:1 & 19**

⁶ For, lo, I raise up the **Chaldeans, that bitter and hasty nation**, which shall march through the breadth of the land, to possess the dwellingplaces that are not their's. **Hab. 1:6**

Here again take note of the land region called Babylon or Chaldea. It's quite clear, **it is in Iraq** (see maps). Thus a future king of Babylon will arise, for the prophecy still has a future installment.

King of Assyria

¹⁸ Thy shepherds slumber, **O king of Assyria**: thy nobles shall dwell in the dust: thy people is scattered upon the mountains, and no man gathereth them. **Nahum 3:18**

I will punish the fruit of the stout heart of the **king of Assyria**, and the glory of his high looks. **Isa. 10:12**

Again Iraq is here in view. See **Nahum 3** for further reading. This passage tells of the destruction of Nineveh, the capital of the revived Empire. This destruction of the Assyria's Nineveh has occurred before, but I believe that there is yet a future fulfillment of this prophecy, on a grandeur scale. Yes, for the antichrist will cause a revival of the Nineveh area, as this is where he will base his capital. Interestingly, the ISIS has captured Mosul, which is just on the other side (east) of the Tigris River, across from Nineveh. ISIS, I predict, is laying the foundations for the eventual rise of the antichrist, for out of all these civil wars in Iraq and Syria, will arise a man, who will become the antichrist. Note that this is still within the area of Babylon, which is just further south in Iraq. Notice that Nahum says, "Ethiopia and Egypt were her strength," and "Put [Libya] and Lubim were thy helpers", al la Ezekiel 38:5 that says "Persia, Ethiopia, and Libya with them". So later on, these are part of the horde that comes with Gog to attack Israel. So both writers have these peoples as the antichrist's helpers. This also tells me that Egypt or at least some Egyptians will join the antichrist's band of soldiers that attack Israel in the end-times.

The Little horn

See this in Daniel 7 & 8 visions, already discussed.

King of the North

See this in Daniel 11:21-45, also already discussed.

Likened to a lion

[6] For a nation is come up upon my land, strong, and without number, whose teeth are the teeth of **a lion**, and he hath the cheek teeth of **a great lion**. **Joel 1:6.** Revelation 13 says he (the beast) has the mouth of a lion. This suggest that he will speak from Nineveh, Iraq, or Mosul, as the lion is a symbol of Iraq.

Idol shepherd

This is from the Hebrew word **Elil** which means good for nothing.

[17] Woe to the **idol shepherd** that leaveth the flock! the sword shall be upon his arm, and upon his right eye: his arm shall be clean dried up, and his right eye shall be utterly darkened. **Zech.11:17.**

It seems that at some point the antichrist will suffer some serious injuries to both one of his arms and his right eye. At this point he seems to be in Jerusalem, hinted at in verse 17.

The Prince of Tyre

[2] Son of man, say unto **the prince of Tyrus**, Thus saith the Lord God; Because thine heart is lifted up, and thou hast said, I am a God, I sit in the seat of God, in the

midst of the seas; yet thou art a man, and not God, though thou set thine heart as the heart of God: **Ezek. 28:2.**

Tyre was and still is a city in the country of Lebanon. Could this be the antichrist's birthplace? It's interesting that all the other place names of the antichrist point to the country of Iraq and/or maybe a part of Iraq and Syria depending on how one looks at it, EXCEPT this one name. I believe this will be the case. It seems to show, via Daniel 11:21 & 23, that he will not be from the region or country that he comes to rule, that is, he was not born there, but will fit in easily due to his Middle Eastern heritage and of course through flattery and deceit. Or perhaps he is of Lebanese heritage, that is, his parents are from Lebanon, but he is born and brought up in another country. This would make him a citizen of Lebanon, by parentage. A father, who is a Lebanese citizen, can as a citizen confer the right of citizenship on his child, and many countries do allow citizenship by parentage and not by birthplace. One thing is clear is that he will be back in the Middle East to assume his role as the future antichrist, if in fact he is not born there.

The Northern Army

But I will remove far off from you **the northern army**, and will drive him into a land barren and desolate, with his face toward the east sea, and his hinder part toward the utmost sea, and his stink shall come up, and his ill savour shall come up, because he hath done great things. **Joel 2:20.**

The antichrist will be the leader of this army. Notice that it's the army being removed at first, then a "him" is driven to a barren and desolate land. It speaks of the leader of the army. Read these chapters 2 & 3 to see the end-time language being used by Joel. Just be clear though on the style of prophecy writers, where verses are mixed up, with information not placed in chronological order. For example, Joel 2 could be read in this order for proper understanding: vs. 12-19, 28-29, 3-9, 1-2, 10-11, and 20-27. Writers such as Daniel, Ezekiel,

Isaiah, Joel and John in Revelation use this same technique, that of setting the stage upfront and then filling in details as they go along. Or they may give a brief outline and then explain with more details later on, with details overlapping. You have to be very aware of this when studying prophecy or you may become confused. The reading as it is in the text, will jump from one scene to another, in the same chapter, and even in the same verse where colons and semi-colons separate the scenes. One must therefore take careful note of colons (:) and semi-colons (;) and full-stops (.), that is why I said earlier that you must read slowly, especially when studying prophecy.

Gog

Therefore, thou son of man, prophesy against **Gog**, and say, Thus saith the Lord GOD; Behold, I am against thee, o **Gog**, the chief prince of Meshech and Tubal: **Ezek. 39:1.**

Read **Ezek. 39** to see the story of Gog's frantic attack on the land of Israel, and how God destroys him and his horde quite easily. The land of Gog is said to have been within the land regions of Iraq and Iran, though some maps put it in south-central Turkey. Look at where the attack takes place – **"upon the mountains of Israel".** In **chap 39,** it says, **"Thou shalt fall upon the mountains of Israel, thou, and all thy bands, and the people that is with thee."** Now take a look at **Isaiah 14:25** that says, **"That I will break the Assyrian in my land, and upon my mountains tread him under foot."** This is still on the mountains of Israel, a term used to denote the general region that the battle will take place. It's not two different battles on the mountains of Israel but the same battle for other Isaiah texts prove it. Notice the end-time terminologies of the Isaiah texts and of Ezekiel. Look at the texts below of Isaiah, and see the Lord saying that HE will perform his whole work (which speaks of completion) on Israel [clearly this is Jacob's trouble and then Armageddon's destruction of the antichrist]. Then later on HE says it's the set purpose on the whole earth....for this is what the whole earth is going towards, Armageddon – the final and utter end of man's rebelliousness against God for this age, and God's complete takeover and recovery of all HIS people, both Jew and Gentile, for "for the Son of man has come to seek and to save that which was lost", **Luke 19:10**. See the texts below:

"that when the Lord hath performed his whole work upon mount Zion and on Jerusalem, I will punish the fruit of the stout heart of the king of Assyria." Isa.10:12

"This is the purpose that is purposed upon the whole earth." Isa.14:26

These texts of Isaiah and Ezekiel connects both Gog and the Assyrian as being on the mountain of Israel to be destroyed by God. This has never happened to any Assyrian king before, and moreover the end-time terminologies used clearly points the reader to the time of the end. This clearly shows the Assyrian to be the self-same Gog.

Here is the antichrist attacking Israel in his anger. There is also another Armageddon comparison to peruse, this time, that of **Ezekiel 39** and the text of **Revelation 19.** Here it is:

[17] And, thou son of man, thus saith the Lord God; <u>Speak unto every feathered fowl, and to every beast of the field, Assemble yourselves, and come; gather yourselves on every side to my sacrifice that I do sacrifice for you, even a great sacrifice upon the mountains of Israel, that ye may eat flesh, and drink blood.</u>

[18] <u>Ye shall eat the flesh of the mighty, and drink the blood of the princes of the earth, of rams, of lambs, and of goats, of bullocks, all of them fatlings of Bashan.</u>

[19] And ye shall eat fat till ye be full, and drink blood till ye be drunken, of my sacrifice which I have sacrificed for you.

[20] Thus ye shall be filled at my table with horses and chariots, with mighty men, and with all men of war, saith the Lord God. Ezek.39:17-20,

and for comparison:

¹⁷ And I saw an angel standing in the sun; and he cried with a loud voice, <u>saying to all the fowls that fly in the midst of heaven, Come and gather yourselves together unto the supper of the great God;</u>

¹⁸ That ye may <u>eat the flesh of kings, and the flesh of captains, and the flesh of mighty men, and the flesh of horses, and of them that sit on them, and the flesh of all men, both free and bond, both small and great.</u>

¹⁹ And I saw the beast, and the kings of the earth, and their armies, gathered together to make war against him that sat on the horse, and against his army. Rev.19:17-19.

Well only the blind or the stubborn will fail to make the connection here. Our God is so great, that HE foretells the history of mankind before it occurs, but more importantly HE reveals it to all who are able to grasp the information. For no prophecy of the scriptures is learnt by self-interpretation, it must be revealed by God Himself. This is the battle of Armageddon, and God has revealed it to more than one writers in the Bible, but each writer brings it out from a different perspective, and even uses a different name for the antichrist. I believe God does this deliberately to allow those of us who study prophecies as well as to HIS people in general, to know in advance important details about the antichrist, the rapture, etc. Thus, you have to take time out to connect the dots and you cannot if God doesn't direct you. It is almost as if God cloaked these prophecies in different books of the Bible, in such a way that only those who earnestly and carefully study them, will receive the understanding thereof. For more comparison of Armageddon text, read **Zechariah 14.**

Antichrist

There is yet another name of the antichrist, and yes you probably are wondering when I would use this name – the antichrist. Well here it is, the one and only time the word is actually used:

[18] Little children, it is the last time: and as ye have heard that **antichrist** shall come, even now are there many antichrists; whereby we know that it is the last time. **1 John 2:18.**

Man of Sin, son of perdition

[3] Let no man deceive you by any means: for that day shall not come, except there come a falling away first, and that **man of sin** be revealed, the **son of perdition;** **2 Thess. 2:3**

Wicked

[8] And then shall that **Wicked** be revealed, whom the Lord shall consume with the spirit of his mouth, and shall destroy with the brightness of his coming: **2 Thess. 2:8**

The Beast

The antichrist is called the beast many times in Revelation, in chapters 13, 14, 15, 16, 17, 19, & 20. I will take two picks, that of Rev. 13 & 19.

[11] And the beast that was, and is not, even he is the eighth, and is of the seven, and goeth into perdition. Rev. 13:11.

[19] And I saw the beast, and the kings of the earth, and their armies, gathered together to make war against him that sat on the horse, and against his army. Rev. 19:19.

Thus, bearing in mind all the various names that refers to the antichrist, the antichrist will rise among the ten horns of the latter day ten nations Muslim/Islamic League of nations and will become the eighth Empire, which is of the seventh [the Ottoman Islamic Empire]. So it appears that just prior to this revived 8th Empire, we will see a round number of ten nations in a coalition, or a pact being formed among them, a Confederacy. These nations will be at their heart, all Muslim nations, and this pact will likely be for one main reason, the ultimate defeat and obliteration of the nation of Israel from the face of the earth, to re-capture and to make Jerusalem their capital. Indeed, former Iranian President Mahmoud Ahmadinejad said, that "the Zionist regime [Israel] is on its way to annihilation and warned that an impending regional storm would uproot Israel from the region." He also stated that Israel had no place in the region. Here's what the Iranian Ayatollah Akbar Hashemi Rafsanjani had to say re Israel, according to The Jewish Press.com, "The presence of the Israeli regime is temporary," Iranian Ayatollah Akbar Hashemi Rafsanjani assured the Hezbollah-linked *Al Ahd* news website in an interview. "Eventually one day this alien forged existence that has been forced into the body of an ancient nation and an historical region will be wiped off the map."

In fact there is tremendous hatred of Israel in the Middle East, and several famous wars have been fought between Israel and its' neighbours, eg, the Six Day War, the 3rd Arab-Israeli war of June 5-10, 1967. They were trying to take over Israel. However Israel will never be defeated as a nation again, with the antichrist being allowed by God to rule over it for just 3 ½ years, before he comes to his defeat at Armageddon. Ezekiel tells us that the Jews will spend seven months burying the enemy's dead, and will burn their weapons for seven years as well as to collect their spoil. This hatred of the Jews can be seen in the actions of Hamas, Hezbollah and many Palestinians, and other Arabs, in the willful attack and killing of the Jews, just because they are Jews and for living in Palestine. The Muslims claim that Palestine belong to them and that the Jews are occupiers. So at the time of the end, many nations will be up against Israel, for Jerusalem will be the envy of them. From the very beginning the antichrist will be against Israel, and the holy covenant, though he will disguise it from the Jews, as well as the world, at least for the first 1130 days or so of the Week, since he will set up the Abomination at 1230 days at the Temple, just before the 1260 days point is reached.

Daniel said that the antichrist will act against the holy covenant with those whom he will corrupt by flatteries, this may or may not include some Jews, but will certainly include those Muslims who join with him. Their hatred for Israel will make this easy so to do. In his rise to power, the antichrist is said to uproot three of the ten nations that were aligned together before his rise. Recall that he comes up among the ten, which means he rises between the borders or straddling the borders of more than one of the country in the league of ten. Or perhaps a country within a country. When I had reached the full understanding of this part of the prophecy, I predicted (while looking at the Iraqi situation, post US led war on Iraq) that this new country would probably come from among the ethnic group, the Kurds. For the Kurds occupy a rough circle of land space straddling four of the **key countries, namely, Iraq, Iran, Syria and Turkey**. This I believed was an ideal area for a new country to rise seeing as how the Kurds were agitating for their own independent homeland. I believed then that an impending war of independence was imminent. This never materialized (although the Kurds still seek independence, and this could therefore still occur), but in the same line of thinking, along came ISIS and has now captured vast swathes of land straddling both Iraq and Syria, including some of the Kurdish areas.

This area, which interestingly and importantly includes Mosul in Iraq, is where I expect the antichrist to eventually rise and assume control. The ISIS already call this area their State, thus a new country is being established by ISIS. Whether they can make it official is another thing, what with the international objection to them. Something though will occur in time to come that will allow the antichrist to enter by flattery and deceit and take over and rule this new country that will certainly come up near the time of the end. Daniel states that he will start small and grow big quickly. So the country will start small at first and the antichrist will assume control over it. That is why I said earlier that ISIS is creating the perfect situation for his rise, as well as he could be in the background pulling the very strings of what is happening here. Then at the appointed and opportune time he will make his move to take control, for he will be a dictator, and such a person wants complete control of affairs. After his rise to power, he will uproot three of the nations, which means that he will overthrow their leaders or leadership, for not going with his agenda, for he cannot physically remove the nations. However, he may cause a change in the lines of their boundaries or borders. His agenda will include the complete control of Israel and ultimately the world. Yes, he thinks BIG.

It is my belief that as per Psalm 83, that a future Middle East war is on the horizon and fast approaching. The nations immediately surrounding Israel will unite to attack Israel one more time. These peoples described in Psalm 83 come from the nations of Lebanon, some of Iraq, the Palestinians of Gaza, some of Egypt, Syria, Saudi Arabia and Jordan (research the old names used here). They will unite to wipe Israel off the face of the earth, but they will be defeated badly by Israel. This is exactly what many Muslims of the region are saying today. Could it be Iran who first attacks Israel, who then responds, only to see the Iranian proxy armies like Hamas and Hezbollah incite the other Muslims to join the fray? Something though, will occur that will cause radical Muslims to want to attack Israel. I believe it will likely have to do with the Temple Mount. Will Israel completely take over the Temple Mount at a future date? Perhaps. I believe that this will ultimately happen. The Jews are determined to build their third Temple on Temple Mount and even Arabs are actually accusing them of wanting to do this and in the process destroy the Al-Aqsa Mosque. The Muslims view the Temple Mount as the 3rd holiest site in Islam, but the Jews regard it as the holiest site in Judaism. Muslims believe Muhammad ascended from there to heaven. They may attack and sabotage the Mount, either by a planted bomb, or maybe a suicide bombing, and the Israelis will respond by completely assuming authority for the area.

Thus their passions will be greatly inflamed and a quick confederacy will be formed and an attack on Israel will occur. Or it could be something else altogether, like Israel taking over more lands in the West Bank, say in Hebron, for example. Anyway, I believe that it will likely be the Jews taking complete control of the Temple Mount and building the third Temple or at least erecting the Altar of sacrifice to resume animal sacrifice. They may even forbid the entry of all Muslims unto the Temple Mount. Psalm 83 tells the story of the attack. The Temple area is currently managed by the Muslims through the Waqf, but Israel has control of the area, for it is part of the Old City which has been in Israeli control since 1967. I believe even ISIS may be in this war, but from its aftermath, which will see Israel emerge victorious, the antichrist will stride forward. This war may even include some nuclear weapons by both sides in the conflict, but as can be seen in the Psalm 83, the enemies of Israel are decisively defeated, with Damascus of Syria being flattened and utterly destroyed in a day according to Isaiah. I believe this act on Damascus will occur during this war. Here's what Isaiah 17 states:

The burden of Damascus. Behold, Damascus is taken away from being a city, and it shall be a ruinous heap.

And behold at eveningtide trouble; and before the morning he is not. Isa. 17:1 & 14.

So this Middle East War is what I expect next to occur, and afterwards, the time will be perfect to see the antichrist rise to perhaps promote peace (a false peace) between those Muslims left alive and Israel. I wish to point out though that the antichrist may in fact never sign any peace treaty with the Jews, but instead sign a treaty with the remaining radical Muslims to bide their time and completely annihilate Israel at a further, appropriate time. Note this man when he comes forth, for he will be against Israel from the beginning, but will use deceit and peaceful overtures to distract them from his real purpose. This Psalm 83 war will see the Jews regain complete control of the Temple Mount area, and the Jews will resume Temple sacrifices, as occurred by the Torah. This may involve the building of a new Temple, but may not necessarily be the case. Instead it could be the Jews just create a holy place (an altar?) within a Tabernacle to offer their animal sacrifices unto God. They have already built many of the Temple implements, inclusive of Priestly garments and an Altar, and have trained Priests to perform same rites and ceremonies according to the Torah. After several other wars against Egypt and other countries which he will take over (1st half of Week?), the antichrist will then turn his attention to Jerusalem. He will attack after about three years (1080 days) or so, and his army will surround Jerusalem maybe for about 40 days, during which time the city will run out of food and water.

Luke 21 hints at this, for he says that "**when ye shall see Jerusalem compassed with armies, then know that the desolation thereof is nigh.**" They will likely heap up earth against the city walls and eventually storm the city and set up the Abomination. This is hinted at by **Habakkuk 1:10, "And they shall scoff at the kings, and the princes shall be a scorn unto them: they shall deride every strong hold; for they shall <u>heap dust</u>, and take it.**" Verses 6-11 tells how the antichrist will attack many nations, or certainly, many of the nations of the world. Those who did not flee as per Jesus' warning, will suffer greatly at the hands of the antichrist and his soldiers, with rape, pillage and killings being the order of the day. Some will even be sold into slavery or sent away to other nations (exiled). The chapter on the Remnant will give more details on this situation. The antichrist will not remain in Jerusalem for the full period of the last 3 ½ years, as his attention will be needed elsewhere. But after setting up himself to be worshipped as God, he will by the false prophet set up an idol/statue of himself at the Temple and command that it be worshipped, or suffer death. He will probably head off to someplace in Europe (Turkey, Rome?) or to North Africa to capture other lands or just to oversee other business. He will leave a sub-commander to be in charge of Israel. He will also divide the land for a profit, perhaps giving Gaza and pre-1967 Israel (West Bank, East Jerusalem & the Golan Heights) back to the Muslims/Palestinians. Israel had captured these areas from the Arabs in the 6 Day War of 1967, against Egypt, Syria and Jordan. After the war, the Israeli Government inexplicably decided to use the liberated land to offer in exchange for peace instead of declaring full sovereignty. That policy has come back to haunt Israel, with the several Intifadas and other Arab terror wars fought against Israel, with the Arabs clamouring for the return of these lands and the Temple Mount.

Thus when his reign is over, he will not be in Iraq when the kings of the East attack and destroy his kingdom in Iraq, with his headquarters at probably Mosul-Nineveh. Daniel 11:43b-44 hints at this: **"and the Libyans and the Ethiopians shall be at his steps. 44. But tidings out of the east and out of the north shall trouble him: therefore he shall go forth with great fury to destroy, and utterly to make away many."** So Daniel 11, v40 up shows the antichrist attacking several nations and conquering them, except Jordan, and thus will not be in Iraq when the kings of the East come calling. The kings of the East will then storm across the dried up River Euphrates in Iraq (see Rev. 16:12) and come towards Jerusalem to fight the armies of the antichrist. The kings of the East may be the army of China alone, or may include other armies from Japan, India, North & South Korea, Vietnam and Bangladesh. Russia's army will likely be the one from the north. Meanwhile, the antichrist, the devil (dragon) and the false prophet by means of the unclean spirits, will seduce them into joining them instead, to go to Israel to the battle of Armageddon. For God will not allow this battle to take place in Jerusalem but will cause this war to be fought in the mountains north of Jerusalem, which Joel calls the valley of Jehoshaphat.

I will also gather all nations, and will bring them down into the valley of Jehoshaphat, and will plead with them there for my people and for my heritage Israel, whom they have scattered among the nations, and parted my land. Joel 3:2

So according to Joel, the antichrist will divide the land of Israel, whereas Daniel 11 says he shall divide the land for gain [for monetary rewards, perhaps or for oil already found in Israel?].

Finally here is the route the antichrist and his soldiers take towards Jerusalem when they attack just prior to setting up the Abomination.

Yes, it is right there in the Bible, revealed to Isaiah by God. It is very interesting that the route taken by the antichrist seeks to avoid the areas controlled by the Jews in the general region of the West Bank and instead seek to travel through the Palestinian controlled communities. Isaiah uses the old Biblical names of the areas, for there were no Palestinians around then, yet God who knows the future showed HIS superiority to humans by telling history before it occurs. HE knew exactly what the situation would be like unto, at the time of the end. This section here was revealed to me by a servant of the Lord, an online friend, from his book, and he has the maps to show it. Here is the passage:

[27] And it shall come to pass in that day, that his burden shall be taken away from off thy shoulder, and his yoke from off thy neck, and the yoke shall be destroyed because of the anointing.

[28] He [the antichrist] is come to Aiath, he is passed to Migron; at Michmash he hath laid up his carriages: [29] They are gone over the passage: they have taken up their lodging at Geba; Ramah is afraid; Gibeah of Saul is fled.

[30] Lift up thy voice, O daughter of Gallim: cause it to be heard unto Laish, O poor Anathoth. [31] Madmenah is removed; the inhabitants of Gebim gather themselves to flee. [32] As yet shall he remain at Nob that day: he shall shake his hand against the mount of the daughter of Zion, the hill of Jerusalem. Isa.10:27-32.

So there you have it. The passage tells how the various citizens react to the antichrist's passage through their towns. Thus, the antichrist is called by various names in the Bible; his rise to power, his actual reign as antichrist in the second part of the Week, 1260 days/3 ½ yrs/42 months, and his eventual destruction at Armageddon are well documented. We should therefore be able to see and know him from sometime during the first 1260 days/3 ½ yrs/42 months, and thus be more prepared to set up areas of tribulation retreats by God's help and direction. For make no mistake, the antichrist through his agents will persecute Christians severely, on a worldwide scale, to force us to accept the mark of the beast in the second part of the

Week. Some Christians will be caught and killed, while others will be betrayed by family members and friends, for a morsel of bread, and for so called security of life. Some will accept the mark and turn their backs on Christ, while many who know their God, will resist even to the death, and do great wonders.

For more reading, see **Hab. 1:5-11**, and **Zech. 11:15-17.**

3   The Remnant

The question of who will be the remnant of Israel, and how they will come about, will be answered in this chapter. Some people believe that a set of saints will come out of the great tribulation as different from the raptured, and will be saved by Christ. They believe that the remnant from the Jews will be those who flee Jerusalem to what many believe will be Petra in Jordan.

I have already settled the issue of the tribulation saints in chapter one (The Rapture), for the rapture will take place at the last trump (1 Cor.15:52), the said such called by John in Rev. 11:15-19, as the seventh trumpet. **It is all who come through the Great Tribulation, that may rightly be regarded as tribulation saints, though it must be noted that all saints through-out history go through some form of tribulation.** Many saints will not be killed by the antichrist and his agents, and also WILL NOT take the mark of the beast during the tribulation. Those who will die for Christ's sake, at the hands of the antichrist, will be taken up in the rapture as well, as Paul said in 1 Thess. 4:13-17. The dead in Christ shall rise first at the trumpet's sound, then we who remain alive up to that point in time, will also then be caught up to be with the Lord. Therefore all the saints who have died from Adam and up to the Week, to those who will die at the hands of the antichrist or from other causes during the Week (so long as they do not take the mark of the beast), will all awaken at the last trump. All Jews alive, who are in the Church will also be caught up in the rapture. **The issue of the remnant therefore, is not in view with regards to the rapture, in so far as the contextual meaning of the words remnant and rapture imply.**

The **remnant** as discussed here, and as pertains to the end-times, **is strictly and only referring to those Jews who survive the time of Jacob's trouble.** This said time period which was discussed earlier, will be 1260days/3 ½ yrs/42 months, during which Israel will be punished by God at the hands of the antichrist, for their rebelliousness to God (**Ezek.39:23**). At the end of this period, which is the second half of the seven year period (the Week), also called the great tribulation, God will save a certain amount of people (Jews only), but who will not be raptured. It is this amount of Jews that are kept alive who are called the remnant – that is, a residue of the people of Israel will be left, who will remain on earth and go into the Millennium, which is the 1000 year rule of Christ on earth. This has nothing to do with those saints who will be taken up in the rapture which includes both Jews and Gentiles, for consider this, who will Christ rule over during the Millennium? Revelation 20:3 & 8 has nations on earth at the expiration of the 1000 years, the question that begs answering then, is, where do these people come from. Are they a new creation? The answer is no. These are the generations of those who did not go up in the rapture, but who remain alive after the battle of Armageddon. It is possible that they may include others apart from Jews, who had not taken the mark of the beast, but neither had accepted Christ as their Saviour. For all who take the mark are doomed, as scripture says, "and he [those who take the mark] shall be tormented with fire and brimstone in the presence of the holy angels, and in the presence of the Lamb: ¹¹ And the smoke of their torment ascendeth up for ever and ever: Rev. 14:10-11. What is sure is that they were not caught up to be with the Lord, for they are not a part of the Elect. To be a part of the Elect, one must be born again, that is, born of water (baptism), and born of the Spirit (Holy Ghost filled). Of course after fulfilling those requirements, one must also be accounted worthy of the rapture, in other words, you must be ready to meet the Lord when HE appears.

Those who enter the Millennium are also not Jews alone, for notice what Zechariah 14 has to say re the aftermath of Armageddon; notice the underlined words, that there are different nations from the Jews still on the earth, and clearly going forward into the Millennium, who go up to Jerusalem to worship the Lord God of hosts.

[11] And <u>men shall dwell in it</u>, and there shall be no more utter destruction; <u>but Jerusalem shall be safely inhabited.</u>

[16] And it shall come to pass, that every one that is left of <u>all the nations</u> which came against Jerusalem <u>shall even go up from year to year to worship the King, the LORD of hosts, and to keep the feast of tabernacles</u>. [17] And it shall be, that whoso will not come up of <u>all the families of the earth</u> unto Jerusalem to worship the King, the LORD of hosts, even upon them shall be no rain.

[18] And if the <u>family of Egypt</u> go not up, and come not, that have no rain; there shall be the plague, wherewith the LORD will smite <u>the heathen</u> that come not up to keep the feast of tabernacles. [19] This shall be the punishment <u>of Egypt</u>, and the punishment <u>of all nations</u> that come not up to keep the feast of tabernacles. Zech.14:11, 16-19.

You will notice however, that these people are not referred to as the remnant, neither are they ever called so by other writers of the Bible. **It is only the Jews that are left alive after the battle of Armageddon, who are called the remnant.** The remnant may also include some of those Jews who were sold into slavery or sent into exile by the antichrist, after the capture of Jerusalem, before Armageddon.

Let's consider some passages that relate to the concept of the remnant, as revealed by God. Here's Zechariah speaking on the matter in chapter 13:

In that day [Day of the Lord/Armageddon] there shall be a fountain opened to the house of David and to the inhabitants of Jerusalem for sin and for uncleanness.

² And it shall come to pass in that day, saith the Lord of hosts, that I will cut off the names of the idols out of the land, and they shall no more be remembered: and also I will cause the prophets and the unclean spirit to pass out of the land. ³ And it shall come to pass, that when any shall yet prophesy, then his father and his mother that begat him shall say unto him, Thou shalt not live; for thou speakest lies in the name of the Lord: and his father and his mother that begat him shall thrust him through when he prophesieth.

⁴ And it shall come to pass in that day, that the prophets shall be ashamed every one of his vision, when he hath prophesied; neither shall they wear a rough garment to deceive: ⁵ But he shall say, I am no prophet, I am an husbandman; for man taught me to keep cattle from my youth. ⁶ And one shall say unto him, What are these wounds in thine hands? Then he shall answer, Those with which I was wounded in the house of my friends.

⁷ Awake, O sword, against my shepherd, and against the man that is my fellow, saith the Lord of hosts: smite the shepherd, and the sheep shall be scattered: and I will turn mine hand upon the little ones. ⁸ And it shall come to pass, that in all the land, saith the Lord, two parts therein shall be cut off and die; but the third shall be left therein. ⁹ And I will bring the <u>third part</u> through the fire, and will refine them as silver is refined, and will try them as gold is tried: they shall call on my name, and I will hear them: I will say, It is my people: and they shall say, The Lord is my God. Zech. 13

From this passage we see God showing that due to the antichrist's attack on Israel, two thirds of the people of Israel will die, but a third shall remain in the land. Of course, it should be noted that these are those who did not heed Jesus' warning to flee Jerusalem or who leave too late and are caught. The third that remain are then sanctified by God (v 9), and these Jews that remain are called the remnant, along with those exiled or sold into slavery. They are the ones who clean up the after-war mess of Armageddon, for seven years.

The prophet Joel also had his say on the matter of the remnant.

³⁰ And I will shew wonders in the heavens and in the earth, blood, and fire, and pillars of smoke. ³¹ The sun shall be turned into darkness, and the moon into blood, <u>before</u> the great and terrible <u>day of the Lord come</u>.

[32] And it shall come to pass, that whosoever shall call on the name of the LORD shall be delivered: for in mount Zion and in Jerusalem shall be deliverance, as the LORD hath said, and in the <u>remnant</u> whom the LORD shall call. Joel 2:30-32

Here is Joel clearly pointing out that those Jews who are delivered from the antichrist by God, are indeed the remnant. Notice this battle (Armageddon) takes place after the cosmic signs, on the Day of the Lord, vs. 30-31. Isaiah proclaimed his version of events also:

[20] And it shall come to pass in that day, that the <u>remnant of Israel</u>, and such as are escaped of the house of Jacob, shall no more again stay upon him[antichrist] that smote them; but shall stay upon the LORD, the Holy One of Israel, in truth. [21] The <u>remnant</u> shall return, even the <u>remnant of Jacob</u>, unto the mighty God.

[22] For though thy people Israel be as the sand of the sea, yet <u>a remnant</u> of them shall return: the consumption decreed shall overflow with righteousness. [23] For the Lord GOD of hosts shall make a consumption, even determined, in the midst of all the land. Isa. 10:20-23.

Notice Isaiah stated that the Lord shall make a consumption [a complete reconstruction] in the midst of all the land, that is, in all of Israel. But again, a remnant shall escape or return.

Now I will go back to Zechariah again, to show that these occurrences are after the Tribulation, and on the day of the Lord/Armageddon.

[9] And it shall come to pass in that day [Day of the Lord/Armageddon], that I will seek to destroy all the nations that come against Jerusalem.

[10] And I will pour upon the house of David, and upon the inhabitants of Jerusalem, the spirit of grace and of supplications: and <u>they shall look upon me whom they have pierced</u>, and they shall mourn for him, as one mourneth for his only son, and shall be in bitterness for him, as one that is in bitterness for his firstborn.

[11] In that day shall there be a great mourning in Jerusalem, as the mourning of Hadadrimmon in the valley of Megiddon. [12] And the land shall mourn, every

Lance Morgan

family apart; the family of the house of David apart, and their wives apart; the family of the house of Nathan apart, and their wives apart;

¹³ The family of the house of Levi apart, and their wives apart; the family of Shimei apart, and their wives apart; ¹⁴ All the families that remain, every family apart, and their wives apart. Zech.12:9-14.

So this is Zechariah confirming Ezekiel's take on the matter of Armageddon. Notice all the nations gather against Jerusalem to destroy it, at least, that is their intention, but they never get to reach Jerusalem. For God destroys them on the mountains of Israel, just north of Jerusalem on the plain of Megiddo. Revelation 14:20 confirms this, **" And the winepress was trodden without the city, and blood came out of the winepress, even unto the horse bridles, by the space of a thousand and six hundred furlongs."** This is the same war of Ezekiel 39, that is led by Gog. Napolean Bonaparte, the French dictator, (1769-1821), called it the most natural battlefield in the world. The word Armageddon is Greek, for the Mount of Megiddo, which is in Israel. The area is also called the valley of Jehoshaphat as well as Esdraelon or Plain/Valley of Jezreel. A great many battles of the Bible have been fought in this general region (eg. Judges 6-7), as well as battles not recorded in the Bible. Example, in 1799 Napoleon Bonaparte defeated a numerically superior Mohammedan army on the plain of Jezreel, this compared to his army of 4000. So only at the appearance of Jesus Christ, as shown, will the Jews finally understand that HE came unto them before but they had rejected HIM as a nation. For **"they shall look upon me whom they have pierced, and they shall mourn for him."** See maps of the Armageddon region on pg. However, after the battle of Armageddon, there are families of the tribes that remain. This is the remnant.

Zechariah tells us that in Jerusalem, at the point of the antichrist's attack with his Muslim troops, there will be chaos. For half the city will go into captivity, and the rest of the people will be left.

Behold, the day of the LORD cometh, and thy spoil shall be divided in the midst of thee.

² For I will gather all nations against Jerusalem to battle; and the city shall be taken, and the houses rifled, and the women ravished; and half of the city shall go forth into captivity, and the residue of the people shall not be cut off from the city. Zech. 14:1-2.

The antichrist's troops will pillage, rape women, and kill many people. Whereas Ezekiel 5:2 & 12, says that a third of the Jews in the city will die by famine and pestilence, a third by the sword and a third will be scattered with the sword after them [those who escape or is exiled]; Zechariah 13:8 says **"two parts therein shall be cut off and die; but the third shall be left therein"**; There is no confusion here. Many Jews will die, two thirds, but a third will be saved from which the remnant will come. If the writers speak mainly of Jerusalem being surrounded, attacked and conquered, then this is true for the whole land of Israel. However, since Zechariah says that half the city will go into captivity, then it stand to reason that other peoples besides Jews will be deported [exiled]. This is acceptable to me, as there are currently many Arabs and peoples of other nationality living in Jerusalem and in the rest of Israel.

Jeremiah also has his take on the matter of Israel's siege by the antichrist.

⁴ And these are the words that the LORD spake concerning Israel and concerning Judah. ⁵ For thus saith the LORD; We have heard a voice of trembling, of fear, and not of peace.

⁶ Ask ye now, and see whether a man doth travail with child? wherefore do I see every man with his hands on his loins, as a woman in travail, and all faces are turned into paleness? ⁷ Alas! for that day is great, so that none is like it: it is even the time of Jacob's trouble, but he shall be saved out of it. Jer. 30:4-7.

So the time period as noted before, called the time of Jacob's trouble, which will be for 3 ½ years, will be the period of time that Israel will be ruled over by the antichrist. Daniel says he shall divide the land, perhaps between those Jews left and the Arabs. This is what the

Palestinians are now asking for, that they be given the land as it was from the 1967 borders of Israel. This land was captured [I prefer recaptured] by Israel from Jordan and Egypt in its war with the Arabs in 1967. Note that Jeremiah says that Israel shall be saved out of it, this does not mean all of Israel however, but a portion, or a remnant. The Apostle Paul confirms this in his Epistle to the Romans. See the next map of the pre-1967 border lines.

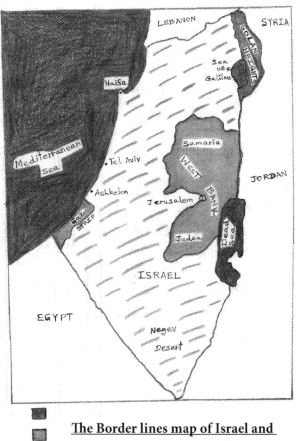

The Border lines map of Israel and surrounding nations of Pre - 1967

The areas of Gaza, and the Samaria-Judea region (called the West Bank), are the disputed areas that the Palestinians want back. This includes East Jerusalem which has the Temple Mount.

Paul also stated that a remnant shall be saved out of Israel.

²⁷ Esaias also crieth concerning Israel, Though the number of the children of Israel be as the sand of the sea, a <u>remnant</u> shall be saved: ²⁸ For he will finish the work, and cut it short in righteousness: because a short work will the Lord make upon the earth. Rom. 9:27-28.

As well as:

²⁵ For I would not, brethren, that ye should be ignorant of this mystery, lest ye should be wise in your own conceits; that blindness in part is happened to Israel, until the fulness of the Gentiles be come in. ²⁶ And so all Israel shall be saved: as it is written, There shall come out of Sion the Deliverer, and shall turn away ungodliness from Jacob: ²⁷ For this is my covenant unto them, when I shall take away their sins. Rom. 11:25-27.

As stated before, it is not all of Israel that will be saved, that is, not every single soul, but a remnant of the people will be saved. It could be that out of every tribe will come a remnant to make the total whole. Revelation 14 shows this principle with the sealing of the 144 000, with 12000 out of every tribe. This 144 000 is not the remnant though, as these are sealed before Armageddon, as they are the first-fruits unto God and to the Lamb. The remnant of Israel are those Jews who survive the battle of Armageddon, that are not caught up in the rapture, and who will enter into the Millennium, living on earth. The new heaven and the new earth will come into being after the 1000 year Millennial rule of Christ on this same earth. These Jews are the ones who Ezekiel points out will clean up the land of Israel of the spoils of the aftermath of the battle of Armageddon.

The Jerusalem War

The war that takes place in and around Jerusalem at the time of the antichrist's attack, said attack beginning at perhaps around the 1160-1200 days point of the first half of the week, will be utterly devastating. The Bible in Ezekiel seems to me to show Jerusalem being surrounded and besieged for 40 days, before the antichrist's troops break through and devastate the city, then causing the Abomination of Desolation. The antichrist's route is already shown at the end of chapter 2 but will be repeated here for emphasis. It is very important to note this route.

[27] And it shall come to pass in that day, that his burden shall be taken away from off thy shoulder, and his yoke from off thy neck, and the yoke shall be destroyed because of the anointing. [28] He [the antichrist] is come to Aiath, he is passed to Migron; at Michmash he hath laid up his carriages: [29] They are gone over the passage: they have taken up their lodging at Geba; Ramah is afraid; Gibeah of Saul is fled.

[30] Lift up thy voice, O daughter of Gallim: cause it to be heard unto Laish, O poor Anathoth. [31] Madmenah is removed; the inhabitants of Gebim gather themselves to flee. [32] As yet shall he remain at Nob that day: he shall shake his hand against the mount of the daughter of Zion, the hill of Jerusalem. <u>Isa.10:27-32.</u>

See the map on next page.

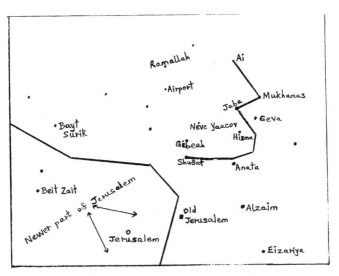

<u>**The route of the antichrist to Jerusalem,
see the line from Ai to Shufat.**</u>

From Shufat, it's a short distance southwards to Old Jerusalem, perhaps to the Western (Wailing) Wall.

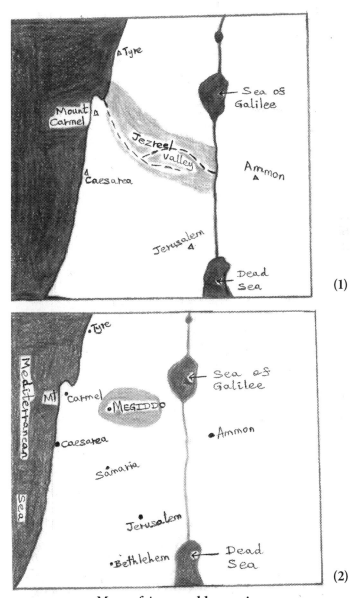

Maps of Armageddon region

Notice that the Jezreel valley (map 1, also called valley of Jehoshaphat), and Megiddo on map 2, are the same region or plain.

Upon reaching the precincts of old Jerusalem (where the Temple Mount is), from following this complicated route, the troops will surround the city, whose walls are about 40 feet tall. According to Wikipedia, the free encyclopedia, Sultan Suleiman I ordered the walls rebuilt during the Ottoman Empire's reign. The effort took four years from 1537-1541, with the wall having a height of 40 feet, the circumference is about 2.4 miles and a width of approximately 8 feet. There are many watchtowers and several gates in the city walls to allow access. The Old City of Jerusalem consists of four quarters, inclusive of a Jewish, Muslim and Christian quarter. The current city of Jerusalem is much larger than the Old City. You can therefore appreciate the difficulties the antichrist soldiers will face in trying to breach the city walls. Isaiah hints that the Jews will actually be at the walls resisting the antichrist's soldiers, perhaps by use of gunfire or other devices to halt his advance, but they will ultimately be defeated, after 40 days. The Muslim quarter has as part of its land area, a section that faces the northern section of the Temple Mount. I believe the antichrist may very well attack through this section and arrive at the wall.

Isaiah says that the antichrist 'remains in Nob this day'….this seems to be the present day Arab community of Shufat, which is approx. 2-3 miles away and just slightly north east of the Old City. Ezekiel 4 and 5 tells what preface the actual war, and some of the things that will occur during the siege and eventual capture of the city of Jerusalem.

Thou also, son of man, take thee a tile, and lay it before thee, and pourtray upon it the city, even Jerusalem: [2] And lay siege against it, and build a fort against it, and cast a mount against it; set the camp also against it, and set battering rams against it round about. [3] Moreover take thou unto thee an iron pan, and set it for a wall of iron between thee and the city: and set thy face against it, and it shall be besieged, and thou shalt lay siege against it. This shall be a sign to the house of Israel.

[4] Lie thou also upon thy left side, and lay the iniquity of the house of Israel upon it: according to the number of the days that thou shalt lie upon it thou shalt bear

their iniquity. ⁵ For I have laid upon thee the years of their iniquity, according to the number of the days, three hundred and ninety days: so shalt thou bear the iniquity of the house of Israel.

⁶ And when thou hast accomplished them, lie again on thy right side, and thou shalt bear the iniquity of the house of Judah forty days: I have appointed thee each day for a year. ⁷ Therefore thou shalt set thy face toward the siege of Jerusalem, and thine arm shall be uncovered, and thou shalt prophesy against it. ⁸ And, behold, I will lay bands upon thee, and thou shalt not turn thee from one side to another, till thou hast ended the days of thy siege. Ezek. 4:1-8

See chap. 5 below:

And thou, son of man, take thee a sharp knife, take thee a barber's razor, and cause it to pass upon thine head and upon thy beard: then take thee balances to weigh, and divide the hair. ² Thou shalt burn with fire a third part in the midst of the city, when the days of the siege are fulfilled: and thou shalt take a third part, and smite about it with a knife: and a third part thou shalt scatter in the wind; and I will draw out a sword after them. ³ Thou shalt also take thereof a few in number, and bind them in thy skirts. ⁴ Then take of them again, and cast them into the midst of the fire, and burn them in the fire; for thereof shall a fire come forth into all the house of Israel. ⁵ Thus saith the Lord GOD; This is Jerusalem: I have set it in the midst of the nations and countries that are round about her.

⁶ And she hath changed my judgments into wickedness more than the nations, and my statutes more than the countries that are round about her: for they have refused my judgments and my statutes, they have not walked in them. ⁷ Therefore thus saith the Lord GOD; Because ye multiplied more than the nations that are round about you, and have not walked in my statutes, neither have kept my judgments, neither have done according to the judgments of the nations that are round about you; ⁸ Therefore thus saith the Lord GOD; Behold, I, even I, am against thee, and will execute judgments in the midst of thee in the sight of the nations. ⁹ And I will do in thee that which I have not done, and whereunto I will not do any more the like, because of all thine abominations.

¹⁰ Therefore the fathers shall eat the sons in the midst of thee, and the sons shall eat their fathers; and I will execute judgments in thee, and the whole remnant of thee will I scatter into all the winds. ¹¹ Wherefore, as I live, saith the Lord GOD; Surely, because thou hast defiled my sanctuary with all thy detestable things, and with all thine abominations, therefore will I also diminish thee; neither shall mine eye spare, neither will I have any pity.

[12] **A third part of thee shall die with the pestilence, and with famine shall they be consumed in the midst of thee: and a third part shall fall by the sword round about thee; and I will scatter a third part into all the winds, and I will draw out a sword after them.** [13] **Thus shall mine anger be accomplished, and I will cause my fury to rest upon them, and I will be comforted: and they shall know that I the LORD have spoken it in my zeal, when I have accomplished my fury in them. Ezek. 5:1-13.**

Here is Ezekiel being commanded by God to take a tile and portray the city of Jerusalem on it. He is to set a siege against it, with v4 suggesting that the siege be for 40 days (a little over a month). The siege will involve a mount being built against it, and battering rams. This is the style of war used to overthrow walled cities of old, that is, siege mounts and battering rams were fully in vogue. Habakkuk 1:10 in speaking of the antichrist army says, [10] **And they shall scoff at the kings, and the princes shall be a scorn unto them: they shall deride every strong hold; <u>for they shall heap dust, and take it</u>.** I believe this is exactly what will happen. The antichrist troops will surround Jerusalem for 40 days before they are able to enter it, due to the Jews defending the city (**Isa.22**). They will build siege ramps against the walls when the Jews have exhausted their weaponry supplies, for example, bullets, and many would have died because of starvation.

Isa. 5:1-7; 22:1-19; 28:14-22 and **29:1-3** (please read all) shows what occurs just prior to the city's overthrow as well as the occurrences after the overthrow. Things that occur: the Jews muster a serious fight against the antichrist and his soldiers, perhaps using guns to fire at them from hidden positions behind the wall; some make a death covenant that they will not run but rather fight to the death; the Jews gather water from the lower pool to help fortify the walls of the old city, along with materials from the houses that they break down; the rulers/leaders all run away when the city is about to be taken. At about the day/days just prior to the takeover, they kill sheep and oxen to eat, and drink wine, as they expect to die the next day. At the breach of the walls, some of the people flee to the mountains, and hide in the forests, but many are caught and killed and exiled. It will be utter devastation and pain to all those who are caught. In the end, only a third of the people will be saved (the remnant), according to Ezekiel.

The Two Witnesses

The matter of the two witnesses is intricately involved in the period of the Great Tribulation, which said period as stated before, lasts for the final 1260 days, 42 months, or 3 ½ years of the last seven years (the 70th Week) of regular life on earth, before the Millennium. This is seen from Rev. 11, where the two witnesses are shown to rise and to prophesy for 1260 days. This occurs during the same time as that of the antichrist's rule, which is for 3 ½ years as noted before. John points out that the Gentiles will trod down Jerusalem for 42 months (42x30days), which is a said length of time. In fact it is the same period of time, in other words, the 42 months of the Gentiles or 3 ½ yrs of the antichrist, and the 1260 days of the two witnesses, all coincide in length with perhaps only a matter of a few days separating each period's start and ending. It is my personal belief though, that all three time periods coincide significantly. In fact, the antichrist is the head of the Gentiles, for it is his forces that will occupy and trod down Jerusalem. See the text below re the two witnesses.

But the court which is without the temple leave out, and measure it not; for it is given unto the Gentiles: and the holy city shall they tread under foot forty and two months. ³ And I will give power unto my two witnesses, and they shall prophesy a thousand two hundred and threescore days, clothed in sackcloth. ⁴ These are the two olive trees, and the two candlesticks standing before the God of the earth.

⁵ And if any man will hurt them, fire proceedeth out of their mouth, and devoureth their enemies: and if any man will hurt them, he must in this manner be killed. ⁶ These have power to shut heaven, that it rain not in the days of their prophecy: and have power over waters to turn them to blood, and to smite the earth with all plagues, as often as they will.

⁷ And when they shall have finished their testimony, the beast that ascendeth out of the bottomless pit shall make war against them, and shall overcome them, and kill them. ⁸ And their dead bodies shall lie in the street of the great city, which spiritually is called Sodom and Egypt, where also our Lord was crucified.

⁹ And they of the people and kindreds and tongues and nations shall see their dead bodies three days and an half, and shall not suffer their dead bodies to be put in graves. ¹⁰ And they that dwell upon the earth shall rejoice over them, and make merry, and shall send gifts one to another; because these two prophets tormented them that dwelt on the earth.

¹¹ And after three days and an half the spirit of life from God entered into them, and they stood upon their feet; and great fear fell upon them which saw them. ¹² And they heard a great voice from heaven saying unto them, Come up hither. And they ascended up to heaven in a cloud; and their enemies beheld them. Rev. 11:2-12.

The question is, does the Bible give some insight as to who the two witnesses are? I believe it does. In the book of **Malachi**, there are a few verses that state this fact. In fact **chapter 4:5-6**, God states:

⁵ Behold, I will send you Elijah the prophet before the coming of the great and dreadful day of the LORD: ⁶ And he shall turn the heart of the fathers to the children, and the heart of the children to their fathers, lest I come and smite the earth with a curse.

This day is none other than the Day of the Lord, which occurs right at the end of time (after the 70th WEEK), at the sound of the last trump. Here is Malachi telling us that God will send the prophet Elijah to turn back the peoples' hearts to HIM [God] **before** the Day of the Lord. This Malachi is long after the time of Elijah's reign as prophet, so if he wrote that God will send him back, then God will send back Elijah. Therefore, it stands to reason that Elijah is one of the two witness as he comes for the final 1260 days just **before** the last trump/Day of the Lord. This 1260 days is also during the reign of the antichrist as stated above. This follows the principle of the related end-time prophecies, where what is in the New Testament has its foundation in the Old Testament. So we see Malachi speaking of

Elijah, and although John doesn't call him by name, he gives more details of Elijah's work (and the other witness) during the period before the Day of the Lord. Therefore, it also stands to reason that some hint of who the other witness is, must be in the Old Testament or elsewhere in the Scriptures.

I decided to search for it once the thought occurred to me, and I decided to begin my search from Malachi 1 since chapter 4 is where Elijah is mentioned. I subsequently found it in chapter 3 v 1. Here's what is written there:

1 Behold, I will <u>send my messenger,</u> and <u>he shall prepare the way before me</u>: and the Lord, whom ye seek, shall suddenly come to his temple, <u>even the messenger of the covenant</u>, whom ye delight in: behold, he shall come, saith the Lord of hosts.

Upon reading this text I knew this was it. Since God states that HE will send HIS messenger to prepare the way, and the said messenger is the messenger of the covenant, the only thing that remained is to factor in the time setting. The theme of Malachi is talking about the Day of the Lord – the period just before and after. Thus, since God speaks of the messenger as being <u>the messenger of the covenant</u> then only one person fits that bill, and that's Moses. It was Moses who spoke to God face to face in receiving the Law (the Covenant) for the children of Israel on Mount Sinai. Also God points out that he [Moses] will prepare the way before HIM. Look at what verse 2 states: **"But who may abide the day of his coming?"** This IS CLEARLY SPEAKING OF THE COMING OF THE LORD. Thus the time setting is clearly pre- Day of the Lord, which agrees with **chap. 4:5-6**, as well as **Rev. 11**. Therefore I believe this is speaking of none other but Moses.

I also realized that the text is not correctly punctuated, and should more look like this:

1 Behold, I will <u>send my messenger,</u> and <u>he shall prepare the way before me</u>: and the Lord, whom ye seek, shall suddenly come to his temple; <u>even the messenger</u>

of the covenant, whom ye delight in: behold, he shall come, saith the Lord of hosts.

I was at home in the night whilst reading this. I immediately decided to search some newer Bible versions the next day, and sure enough I found it in the NIV. See below:

"I will send my messenger, who will prepare the way before me. Then suddenly the Lord you are seeking will come to his temple; the messenger of the covenant, whom you desire, will come," says the Lord Almighty. Mal. 3:1, NIV.

I believe that God revealed this to me, HE has given me a gift of understanding of Scriptures that never seizes to amaze me, upon doing the subsequent research after reading and studying. **So I therefore believe that the two witnesses are Moses and Elijah**, who interestingly were also with Christ at the Mount of Transfiguration –**Matt. 17:3** ....the word used is Elias, which is the Greek for Elijah. Their death and resurrection will subsequently occur right before the people –**REV.11:7-12**.

It is important to point out that the story of the two witnesses, ends with their death and resurrection (after 3 days) up to heaven in the sight of the people, followed by a great earthquake which kills 7000 people. This is recorded as the second woe (v.14) and is quickly followed by the third woe, which is the sounding of the seventh trumpet, referred to by Apostle Paul as the last trump in **1 Cor.15:51-53. This is the rapture. However, it is also important to point out that some days will pass between the two witnesses' resurrection and that of the church at the last trump (the end of the 3rd woe). This is explained in the next chapter.**

See the text below, which is a continuation of **Rev. 11: 13-19.** Observe v 18 closely.

[13] And the same hour was there a great earthquake, and the tenth part of the city fell, and in the earthquake were slain of men seven thousand: and the remnant

were affrighted, and gave glory to the God of heaven. [14] The second woe is past; and, behold, the third woe cometh quickly. [15] And the seventh angel sounded; and there were great voices in heaven, saying, The kingdoms of this world are become the kingdoms of our Lord, and of his Christ; and he shall reign for ever and ever. [16] And the four and twenty elders, which sat before God on their seats, fell upon their faces, and worshipped God,

[17] Saying, We give thee thanks, O LORD God Almighty, which art, and wast, and art to come; because thou hast taken to thee thy great power, and hast reigned. [18] And the nations were angry, and thy wrath is come, and the time of the dead, that they should be judged, and that thou shouldest give reward unto thy servants the prophets, and to the saints, and them that fear thy name, small and great; and shouldest destroy them which destroy the earth. [19] And the temple of God was opened in heaven, and there was seen in his temple the ark of his testament: and there were lightnings, and voices, and thunderings, and an earthquake, and great hail.

So the two witnesses are taken up to heaven at the end of the second woe, which is the 6th trumpet. However, even though the Bible says that the next woe occurs quickly after, other things happen before we come to the 3rd and final woe – the 7th trumpet, v. 15. I will speak more on this matter in the next chapter. One other point to note here, the two witnesses are called by God as, 'These are the two olive trees, and the two candlesticks standing before the God of the earth.' The same is said in Zech. 4:2-3 & vs12-14, with Zechariah calling them the 'two anointed ones.' Obviously these are not members of the Jewish remnant or of the Church, nor angelic beings of the order of say, Michael, for example. These and other angels have other specific tasks. John also saw them as the olive trees just like Zechariah. I believe they are Moses and Elijah anointed by God to carry out the specific work of the two witnesses at the time of the end. Elijah was caught up alive (2 Kings2:11) and Moses must have been resurrected (see Moses death and burial in Deut. 34:5-7), for satan contended with Michael over his body, Jude v 9. Satan may have resisted the raising of Moses to eternal life on the grounds of Moses' sin at Meribah **(Deut.32:51)**, and his murder of the Egyptian **(Exodus 2:12).** After all, he is known as the accuser of the brethren. Remember that both Moses and Elijah appeared with Jesus at the Mount of Transfiguration. Moreover, during the 1260 days, they perform feats that they both did whilst on earth before, but to a greater degree at the time of the end – they command drought (no rainfall) like Elijah and turn water to blood among other signs, like Moses in Egypt. These are also perhaps Israel's two most foremost prophets.

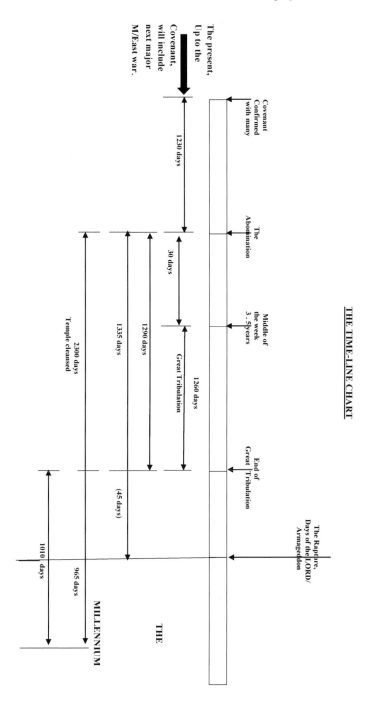

THE TIME-LINE CHART

The present,
Up to the
Covenant,
will include
next major
M/East war.

Covenant
Confirmed
with many

1230 days

The
Abomination

30 days

Middle of
the week
3 . 5years

Great Tribulation

1260 days

1290 days

1335 days

End of
Great Tribulation

2300 days
Temple cleansed

(45 days)

The Rapture,
Days of the LORD/
Armageddon

1010 days

965 days

THE

MILLENNIUM

4

The Order of Revelation's Plagues

THIS IS THE CHAPTER OF ALL CHAPTERS. It will even be controversial to many folks, nevertheless its place in this book is of vital importance. There will be many who will disagree with its written content (i.e. the Order), but **I FIRMLY BELIEVE IT TO BE TRUE, except for a few other details which I will point out.** The written order of the seals, trumpets and plagues given in Revelation is set out in such a way starting with all the seals (**Rev. 6 & 10**), then all the trumpets (**Rev. 8-11**), followed lastly by all the plagues (**Rev. 15-16**). This particular order is commonly called the Consecutive Order. A really close look at the written order however (the Consecutive Order) presents several problems that can become confusing, and God is not the author of confusion. Before I go into the matter though I must point out how I came to the order that will be presented here. I had read the order set out in Revelation and like most people simply believed the plagues would occur as written therein. All this happened before I began in-depth end-time studies. A few years after I began studying end-time material and about mid-2014, I came to realize that the contents of Revelation were intricately intertwined in the studies. This was so because I came to realize that John's 7th trumpet was Paul's last trump in 1 Corinthians 15; I also saw that the 6th seal of Rev. 6:12-14, was what Jesus proclaimed to the Apostles in Matt. 24; and I also saw the similarities of Daniel's prophecies with that of John's in Revelation. I knew then that I had to do a more in-depth study of Revelation, more than just the study of Daniel's and John's beastly kingdoms, or that of the antichrist character. Something was gnawing at my spirit, telling me that I was missing something, some revelation as pertaineth to the full understanding of the end-times.

So I began studying Revelation from chapter 1 in a more systematic way. I soon realized that what I was missing had to do with the plagues. I could not relate their order properly in conjunction with my then understanding and acceptance of a post-tribulational return of the Lord Jesus Christ at the rapture. I read a few books on the End-times but I still was not satisfied – something was still gnawing at my spirit, for even though various writers made a great attempt at explaining the seals, trumpets and plagues, the order was still problematic for me. They were impressive in some of their details though, and I did see some things a little clearer, but my spirit remained unsatisfied. I continued to study the end-time info I had gathered but couldn't figure out exactly what I was missing. **Then suddenly it happened.** I was home one Saturday in late 2014, sitting on my verandah and thinking about the prophecies, when a sudden thought just hit me. **I just felt impressed upon by the Spirit of the Lord to go back into my room and search through a particular stack of printed documents that I had in a certain section of the room**. I immediately got up and went to the exact spot that I was told to do, took up the documents and began searching through them. Why I did it I will never know, but to God be the glory, for I felt it was HIS Spirit that so directed me. I kept looking, knowing that I was going to see something that I did not know was there in that pack of papers, and I also knew that it would be exceedingly important. All this I felt in my spirit, while I was still searching. Suddenly, I saw it. The headlines jumped out at me – "The Order of Revelation's 21 Plagues." I became very excited, and nervous too. **Without a doubt in my mind, I immediately knew this was what the Spirit sent me for.**

I put back the other papers and took that one to the verandah, sat down and began to read. Looking back at it now, I realized that I had seen this document on a website and had without really knowing why, printed it and filed it with some other documents. In fact this document was printed from about 2010, for there were other documents in the file that were so dated. This site belonged to an online writer of whom I am now a big reader and admirer of his work. I began reading some of his work in 2010, yet I did not realize he had written on this subject, until I read the paper at home. **It is his study and the revelation that he got, re the order of the plagues, and I agree with it.** Interestingly I probably would never know that he had written this work as I never ventured to that part of his website where I got this chapter. So it must have been the Lord who caused me to have seen it and printed it from 2010 and filed it away. In any case, at that point in time I was not ready to receive that body of information. The Lord would first have me receive the proper understanding of the linked prophecies of Daniel and John, as well as that of Paul and the Gospels of Matt. 24, Luke 21 and Mark 13.

I read through slowly (about a week), due to the other activities I had, but by page 7, all things fell into place. The final bolt slid home, so to speak. I have re-read it several times since, and as I said before, **I FIRMLY BELIEVE IT TO BE TRUE**. I will use this work to explain the order but will add a few other things, but credit must go to my friend in the Lord, and ultimately to God Himself, for only God could reveal this. Such is the way of the prophecies of the plagues of Revelation. They are expertly hidden by God and take tremendous searching and studying for their unveiling. I must point out too, that through reading from my friend's website, I have had my understanding opened even more with regards to the end-time prophecies. Indeed, I thank him for his permission to use some of his information and as such I give a link to his page here: <u>www.tribwatch.com/updateIraqIndex.htm.</u> You can then look for "The Order of Revelation's 21 Plagues" in the Table of Contents. As he said in the book, a careful analysis of the written order of the seals, trumpets and plagues (called Bowls by writer) reveal that some of the trumpets and plagues occur before the seals; and some of the plagues occurring before the trumpets. This then presents some big problems for the Consecutive Order, for it positions the 7th trumpet at about the midway point of the 70th Week, and as I clearly showed earlier, this is the last trump of Paul in 1 Corinthians 15. By virtue of this 7th trumpet being placed at the midway point by the Consecutive Order, the 6th seal is pushed to the first half of the Week. All of which is incorrect, thus requiring another order. It is this better and correct order that I was missing.

I will not attempt here to rehash other printed material on the order of the seals, trumpets and plagues, but will instead focus on this particular order. I will present the order as written by my friend first and then give corresponding explanations, observations and conclusions thereto. Instead of the order following that of the Consecutive, or otherwise, **the order is a sequential system of triplets where a <u>seal</u> is followed by a <u>trumpet</u>, which in turn is followed by a <u>plague</u>. The sequence is thus read horizontally as follows:**

- **1st Seal, 1st Trumpet, 1st Plague**
- **2nd Seal, 2nd Trumpet, 2nd Plague**
- **3rd Seal, 3rd Trumpet, 3rd Plague**
- **4th Seal, 4th Trumpet, 4th Plague**
- **5th Seal, 5th Trumpet, 5th Plague -- end of 1260 days/3 ½ yrs Tribulation period.**
- **6th Seal (immediately after), 6th Trumpet, 6th Plague**
- **7th Seal, 7th Trumpet (Rapture), 7th Plague ---- Armageddon war.**

These are the triplets combined, I have set them out according to the system above.

THE ORDER IS A SEAL, FOLLOWED BY A TRUMPET, THEN A PLAGUE

Scriptures are taken from the KJV.

1st Seal – Trumpet – Plague

And I saw in the right hand of him that sat on the throne a book written within and on the backside, **sealed with seven seals. Rev. 5:1.**

1And I saw when the Lamb opened **one of the seals,** and I heard, as it were the noise of thunder, one of the four beasts saying, Come and see.

² And I saw, and behold a white horse: and he that sat on him had a bow; and a crown was given unto him: and he went forth conquering, and to conquer. **Rev. 6:1-2 (Seal).**

False religion.

---

⁶ And the seven angels which had the **seven trumpets** prepared themselves to sound.

⁷ **The first angel sounded**, and there followed hail and fire mingled with blood, and they were cast upon the earth: and the third part of trees was burnt up, and all green grass was burnt up. **Rev.8:6-7, (Trumpet).**

And I saw another sign in heaven, great and marvellous, seven angels having **the seven last plagues**; for in them is filled up the wrath of God. **Rev. 15:1.**

² And the **first [angel] went, and poured** out his vial [plague] upon the earth; and there fell a noisome and grievous sore upon the men

which had the mark of the beast, and upon them which worshipped his image. **Rev. 16:2, (Plague).**

2nd Seal – Trumpet - Plague

[3] And when he had opened the **second seal**, I heard the second beast say, Come and see.

[4] And there went out another horse that was red: and power was given to him that sat thereon to take peace from the earth, and that they should kill one another: and there was given unto him a great sword. **Rev.6:3-4, (Seal).**

Wars and more wars.

---

[8] And **the second angel sounded**, and as it were a great mountain burning with fire was cast into the sea: and the third part of the sea became blood;

[9] And the third part of the creatures which were in the sea, and had life, died; and the third part of the ships were destroyed. **Rev. 8:8-9, (Trumpet).**

A massive tsunami (tidal wave) will follow this possible asteroid or a volcanic mountain collapsing into the sea. The tsunami destroys the ships in its wake.

---

[3] And the **second angel poured** out his vial upon the sea; and it became as the blood of a dead man: and every living soul died in the sea. **Rev. 16:3, (Plague).**

3rd Seal – Trumpet - Plague

⁵ And when he had opened the **third seal**, I heard the third beast say, Come and see. And I beheld, and lo a black horse; and he that sat on him had a pair of balances in his hand.

⁶ And I heard a voice in the midst of the four beasts say, A measure of wheat for a penny, and three measures of barley for a penny; and see thou hurt not the oil and the wine. **Rev.6:5-6. (Seal)**

Famine ensues after all the wars and death of some food sources, eg, fishes.

---

¹⁰ And the **third angel sounded**, and there fell a great star from heaven, burning as it were a lamp, and it fell upon the third part of the rivers, and upon the fountains of waters;

¹¹ And the name of the star is called Wormwood: and the third part of the waters became wormwood; and many men died of the waters, because they were made bitter. **Rev. 8:10-11, (Trumpet).**

This certainly seems to be an asteroid (great burning star).

---

⁴ And the **third angel poured** out his vial upon the rivers and fountains of waters; and they became blood. **Rev. 16:4, (Plague).**

4th Seal – Trumpet - Plague

⁷ And when he had opened the **fourth seal**, I heard the voice of the fourth beast say, Come and see.

⁸ And I looked, and behold a pale horse: and his name that sat on him was Death, and Hell followed with him. And power was given unto them over the fourth part of the earth, to kill with sword, and with hunger, and with death, and with the beasts of the earth. **Rev.6:7-8, (Seal).**

---

¹² And the **fourth angel sounded**, and the third part of the sun was smitten, and the third part of the moon, and the third part of the stars; so as the third part of them was darkened, and the day shone not for a third part of it, and the night likewise. **Rev. 8:12, (Trumpet).**

---

⁸ And the **fourth angel poured** out his vial upon the sun; and power was given unto him to scorch men with fire.

⁹ And men were scorched with great heat, and blasphemed the name of God, which hath power over these plagues: and they repented not to give him glory. **Rev.16:8-9, (Plague).**

5th Seal – Trumpet - Plague

⁹ And when he had opened the **fifth seal**, I saw under the altar the souls of them that were slain for the word of God, and for the testimony which they held:

¹⁰ And they cried with a loud voice, saying, How long, O Lord, holy and true, dost thou not judge and avenge our blood on them that dwell on the earth?

¹¹ And white robes were given unto every one of them; and it was said unto them, that they should rest yet for a little season, until their

fellowservants also and their brethren, that should be killed as they were, should be fulfilled. **Rev.6:9-11. (Seal).**

The religious persecution gets more severe.

---

[13] And I beheld, and heard an angel flying through the midst of heaven, saying with a loud voice, Woe, woe, woe, to the inhabiters of the earth by reason of the other voices of the trumpet of the three angels, which are yet to sound! Rev. 8:13.

And the **<u>fifth angel sounded</u>**, and I saw a star fall from heaven unto the earth: and to him was given the key of the bottomless pit.

[2] And he opened the bottomless pit; and there arose a smoke out of the pit, as the smoke of a great furnace; and the sun and the air were darkened by reason of the smoke of the pit.

[3] And there came out of the smoke locusts upon the earth: and unto them was given power, as the scorpions of the earth have power.

[4] And it was commanded them that they should not hurt the grass of the earth, neither any green thing, neither any tree; but only those men which have not the seal of God in their foreheads. [5] And to them it was given that they should not kill them, but that they should be tormented five months: and their torment was as the torment of a scorpion, when he striketh a man.

[6] And in those days shall men seek death, and shall not find it; and shall desire to die, and death shall flee from them.

[12] <u>One woe is past</u>; and, behold, there come two woes more hereafter. **Rev. 9:1-9,12..(Trumpet).**

5 months later:

[10] And the **fifth angel poured** out his vial upon the seat of the beast [antichrist]; **and his kingdom was full of darkness;** and they gnawed their tongues for pain,

[11] And blasphemed the God of heaven because of their pains and their sores, and repented not of their deeds. **Rev. 16:10-11, (Plague).**

The end of the Great Tribulation, for the antichrist's reign comes to an end here. Thus ends the 1260 days, 42 months or 3 ½ years time of Jacob's Trouble. Notice what occurs next at the 6th Seal.

Note: this is not the time that the antichrist is killed.

6th Seal – Trumpet - Plague

[12] And I beheld when he had opened the **sixth seal**, and, lo, there was a great earthquake; and the sun became black as sackcloth of hair, and the moon became as blood;

[13] And the stars of heaven fell unto the earth, even as a fig tree casteth her untimely figs, when she is shaken of a mighty wind.

[14] And the heaven departed as a scroll when it is rolled together; and every mountain and island were moved out of their places. **Rev. 6:12-14. (Seal).**

Compare Matt. 24:29

[29] Immediately [very soon after] **after the tribulation of those days** shall the sun be darkened, and the moon shall not give her light, and

the stars shall fall from heaven, and the powers of the heavens shall be shaken:

[This is the 6th seal described here, the signs are exactly the same, but note that Jesus said they would occur after the tribulation, i.e. at its end].

See also Joel 2:30-31; Luke 21:25; Mark 13:24-25.

---

[14] Saying to the **sixth angel which had the trumpet**, Loose the four angels which are bound in the great river Euphrates. [15] And the four angels were loosed, which were prepared for an hour, and a day, and a month, and a year, for to slay the third part of men.

[16] And the number of the army of the horsemen were two hundred thousand thousand: and I heard the number of them. [17] And thus I saw the horses in the vision, and them that sat on them, having breastplates of fire, and of jacinth, and brimstone: and the heads of the horses were as the heads of lions; and out of their mouths issued fire and smoke and brimstone.

[18] By these three was the third part of men killed, by the fire, and by the smoke, and by the brimstone, which issued out of their mouths. **Rev. 9:14-18, (Trumpet).**

This seems to be military tanks, for horses do not spit fire from their mouths, but John gave the description as he saw it in his time. Such machinery is a twentieth century phenomenon.

Still during the 2nd woe (the 6th Trumpet), but at its ending, after the death of the three witnesses.

¹³ And the same hour was there a great earthquake, and the tenth part of the city fell, and in the earthquake were slain of men seven thousand: and the remnant were affrighted, and gave glory to the God of heaven.

¹⁴ The <u>second woe is past</u>; and, behold, the third woe cometh quickly. **Rev. 11:13-14**

A short while later:

¹² And the **sixth angel poured** out his vial upon the great river Euphrates; and the water thereof was dried up, that the way of the kings of the east might be prepared.

¹³ And I saw three unclean spirits like frogs come out of the mouth of the dragon, and out of the mouth of the beast, and out of the mouth of the false prophet.

¹⁴ For they are the spirits of devils, working miracles, which go forth unto the kings of the earth and of the whole world, to gather them to the battle of that great day of God Almighty. **Rev. 16:12-14, (Plague).**

7th Seal – Trumpet - Plague

And when he had <u>opened the **seventh seal**</u>, there was silence in heaven about the space of half an hour. [I believe this is the prelude to the sounding of the 7th trumpet, thus the silence].

³ And another angel came and stood at the altar, having a golden censer; and there was given unto him much incense, that he should offer it with the prayers of all saints upon the golden altar which was before the throne.

⁴ And the smoke of the incense, which came with the prayers of the saints, ascended up before God out of the angel's hand.

⁵ And the angel took the censer, and filled it with fire of the altar, and cast it into the earth: and there were voices, and thunderings, and lightnings, and an earthquake. **Rev. 8:1, 3-4, (Seal).**

---

⁷ But in the days of the voice of the seventh angel, when he shall begin to sound, the mystery of God should be finished, as he hath declared to his servants the prophets. **Rev.10:7**

¹⁵ And the **seventh angel sounded**; and there were great voices in heaven, saying, The kingdoms of this world are become the kingdoms of our Lord, and of his Christ; and he shall reign for ever and ever.

¹⁸ And the nations were angry, and thy wrath is come, and the time of the dead, that they should be judged, and that thou shouldest give reward unto thy servants the prophets, and to the saints, and them that fear thy name, small and great; and shouldest destroy them which destroy the earth.

¹⁹ And the temple of God was opened in heaven, and there was seen in his temple the ark of his testament: and there were lightnings, and voices, and thunderings, and an earthquake, and great hail. **Rev. 11: 15, 18-19. (Trumpet).**

The end of the third woe. Also the last trumpet and point of rapture of the church. Observe verse 18 above. Compare Matt. 24 below.

³⁰ And then shall appear the sign of the Son of man in heaven: and then shall all the tribes of the earth mourn, and they shall see the Son of man coming in the clouds of heaven with power and great glory.

[31] And he shall send his angels with a **great sound of a trumpet**, and they shall gather together his elect from the four winds, from one end of heaven to the other. **Matt. 24:30-31.**

Also

[51] Behold, I shew you a mystery; We shall not all sleep, but we shall all be changed,

[52] In a moment, in the twinkling of an eye, **at the last trump**: for the **trumpet shall sound**, and the dead shall be raised incorruptible, and we shall be changed. **1 Cor. 15:51-52.**

Also

[16] For the Lord himself shall descend from heaven with a shout, with the voice of the archangel, and with the **trump of God**: and the dead in Christ shall rise first:

[17] Then we which are alive and remain shall be caught up together with them in the clouds, to meet the Lord in the air: and so shall we ever be with the Lord. **1 Thess. 4:16-17.**

See also Mark 13:26-27.

---

[17] And the **seventh angel poured** out his vial into the air; and there came a great voice out of the temple of heaven, from the throne, saying, it is done.

[18] And there were voices, and thunders, and lightnings; and there was a great earthquake, such as was not since men were upon the earth, so mighty an earthquake, and so great. **Rev. 16:17-18, (Plague).**

As I hinted above in the 4th paragraph of this chapter, it was the placement of the 6th Seal of Revelation in the Consecutive Order, or the written order, that had me stymied. You see, this seal portrayed the said same occurrences of **Matt. 24: 29 (see 6th triplet above)**, THAT JESUS EXPRESSLY SAID WOULD OCCUR, **"immediately after the tribulation of those days".** So the 6th Seal tells us what happens **"AFTER"** the Tribulation, which means that the Tribulation has ended. The reader is to note that none of the seven seals say exactly when the Tribulation ends, seal 6 only states what occurs **after.** Therefore if you follow the written order of the seals – trumpets – plagues, you will have to recognize, in view of seal 6, that the end of the Tribulation must be denoted elsewhere in the written order. This clearly will be written either in the trumpets or the plagues, for it is not in the seals. I firmly believe that the Lord would clearly have given notice of the end of the Tribulation period in Revelation, as HE did to Daniel (1290 days), and indeed HE did.

However, let's go back to Daniel to see what he had to say on the matter:

[11] **And from the time that the daily sacrifice shall be taken away, and the abomination that maketh desolate set up, there shall be a thousand two hundred and ninety days. [1290]**

[12] **Blessed is he that waiteth, and cometh to the thousand three hundred and five and thirty days. [1335] Dan. 12:11-12.**

Daniel states that from the time that the daily sacrifice is stopped and the Abomination set up, there will be 1290 days (30 + 1260). As shown on The Timeline Chart in Chapter 3 of the book, this means that this occurs 30 days before the middle of the Week, thus leaving and fulfilling the 1260 days of the second part of the Week. Therefore, it is at the final 30 days of the first 1260 days of the Week (1230 + 30), that the Abomination is set up. Then v12 tells us that at 1335 days, those who waiteth, will be blessed. **That's all of 45 days after**

the Great Tribulation has ended (1335 – 1290). It also means that both time periods start at the same time (see chart). So Daniel clearly shows the G.T. to be 1260 days long, and Rev. 11:2-3, backs this up. In view of all this, what does Revelation say, as to when the tribulation ends, is it specifically in the Trumpets or Plagues? Let's take a look at the 5th triplet. The 5th Seal talks about the great religious persecution that will take place under the antichrist on the body of Christ, where many will be martyred for HIS Names' sake. Jesus explained this in Matt. 24:9-12 & 21-22. Jesus said that if the days were not shortened [limited], then no flesh would be saved, but the days will be limited for the elect's sake. This 5th seal give some more details on the matter.

Next, the seal is followed by the first woe - the 5th Trumpet. I must point out here that after the 4th Trumpet, the three woes correspond to the 5th, 6th and 7th Trumpets. For after the 5th and 6th Trumpet, John states, "the first woe is past", and "the second woe is past", respectively; "and, behold, the third woe cometh quickly." I also arrived at the same conclusion on this as my friend, without having read his book. Therefore, let me quote my online writer from his book, The Order of Revelations 21 Plagues: "The meaning is clear: each Woe equals one trumpet blast. After the details of the 5th Trumpet are given, the text reads, "The first woe is past." After outlining plagues of the 6th Trumpet, as well as the resurrections of the Two Witnesses and the Jerusalem earthquake, the text reads, "The *second woe* has passed. Behold, the *third woe* is coming quickly. The seventh angel sounded his trumpet..." (11:14-15). So then, make no mistake about it, **the third Woe and the 7th Trumpet are one and the same.** And if the second woe is post-tribulational because it includes the Jerusalem earthquake occurring after the deaths of the Two Witnesses, then the subsequent third Woe/7th Trumpet must be more *post-trib* still." But the details of the 5th trumpet/1st woe, state clearly that only those men who have not the seal of God in their foreheads, **will be tormented for 5 months. Observe that this is 5 months, but the trumpet does not say when the tribulation ends either.**

What follows next is the 5th Plague, which comes just before the 6th Seal in the triplet system. I pause here before I go into the details of the 5th plague to share some more from my online writer friend:

TThe 5th Trumpet, because it is said to last for a minimum of 5 months, must be sounded before the opening of the 6th Seal, for there are not five months left in current history after the 6th Seal. All that remains is the post-tribulation period lasting a matter of weeks (Daniel 12:11-12), at most 75 days (I think 45). If the 5th Trumpet cannot occur after the 6th Seal, then a completely new sequential system must be drawn up which places the first five Trumpets before the 6th Seal.

I also have 45 days left after the tribulation for the rest of the order to occur, which is approx. 1 ½ months. For the months I believe will go back to being 30 days each due to the cosmic disturbances. This is the order left after the tribulation:

6th seal, 6th trumpets, 6th plague
7th seal, 7th trumpet, 7th plague.

So then, seal 6 immediately follows the 5th plague in the triplet system. Extrapolating from the book, it stands to reason therefore, that the 5th plague is the one that signifies the very end of the tribulation period, (see triplet chart). Observe what the Bible says, re the 5th plague:

[10] And the <u>fifth angel poured</u> out his vial upon the seat of the beast [antichrist]; <u>and his kingdom was full of darkness;</u> and they gnawed their tongues for pain, [11] And blasphemed the God of heaven because of their pains and their sores, and repented not of their deeds. Rev. 16:10-11.

I agree with the book here. Since the beast gets 42 months/1260 days to trample Jerusalem, Rev. 13:5, then this 5th plague definitely brings the tribulation to its end, and thus it can't be placed after the 42 months has ended. Instead, after the 5 month's action of the locusts of the 5th trumpet, the 5th plague immediately follows and closes out exactly the 1260 days/42 months. Notice that the beast's kingdom is plunged into darkness courtesy of the angel, an act of God signifying closure. However, the antichrist is not killed yet, just that his 1260 day rule is over. His death occurs at the 7th plague – Armageddon. Seal 6 immediately follows the 5th plague. Jesus puts it nicely: **"immediately after the tribulation of those days"**........

If we were to place the 6th seal before the tribulation, then another such occurrence will have to be put into the order, whether it be the Consecutive order or this new triplet order system. Surely there is not two HAPPENINGS of "the sun be darkened, and the moon shall not give her light, and the stars shall fall from heaven, and the powers of the heavens shall be shaken:" It will not happen, that is why I am sure and is in agreement with my friend….Matt. 24:29 and Rev. 6:12-14, are one and the same event. Let there be no confusion, the triplet system punted by my online friend is absolutely brilliant. It satisfies all the queries that arise. Thus I will address from here on in, the occurrences from the 6th seal through to the 7th plague and what follows the last and 7th plague. I will detail the happenings from after the tribulation through to the rapture and beyond.

After the Tribulation

After the tribulation ends, what follows is a frenetic and spectacular set of occurrences, from the 6th seal through to the 7th plague, which occurs over a 45 day period. Look at the comparison above of Matt. 24 and Rev. 6, as it relates to the 6th seal in the triplet system. The same set of occurrences take place (see underlined sections), immediately after the tribulation, that is, at the end of the 1260 days/42 months reign of the antichrist. The 6th trumpet follows quickly afterwards, with the trumpet loosening the four angels that are bound in the great river Euphrates. This river runs from in Turkey, through Syria, then through the country of Iraq, where it joins the river Tigris, which is east of it. They join together in southern Iraq and flow as one into the Persian Gulf. The hour, day, month and year spoken of in v15, speaks to the appointed time of Armageddon, that the army will arrive in Israel.

The angels summon the 200 million man army towards the river, so as to cross it at a particular point. This will require the drying up of the river at that spot, but this does not occur here. All that this 6th trumpet does is summon the army to the river. This is another good proof of the triplet system, for the 6th trumpet MUST occur before the 6th plague, as the trumpet summons the army while the plague does the actual drying up of the river Euphrates. The army will in due course (from its time of fighting) slay a third of mankind, this I agree with my online friend. The dead will include those of the antichrist's army in Iraq, and civilians. There are always civilian casualties in war. It is this army which destroys the antichrist's base of operations (Military HQ), thus helping to bring his reign to an end. However, as noted before, the antichrist will not be in Iraq then, but perhaps in North Africa (Dan. 11:40-44), so his capture or death at the hands of the Kings of the East, who lead the 200 million man army, does not occur here.

The army may well be just horses as John said, but as he saw it so long ago, it may well be military tanks and other modern weapons, for horses do not issue fire, smoke and brimstone out of their mouths, but tanks do via large caliber cannon set on rotating gun turrets. Helicopters do this via missiles. Or peradventure, other modern weapons, nuclear and non-nuclear will be on the scene at the time of the end, that will resemble John's descriptions, you can bet on it. He described the weapons that he saw by using the weapons of his time that he was familiar with, for he could never comprehend those that he saw in the vision. Still, I believe there will be horses at the battle, for this is a Middle Eastern culture, plus Ezekiel (39) like John (Rev.19) saw horses there. The Lord Himself called for the birds of the heavens to come and eat the flesh of horses and of men in both books. Also, the armies of the kings of the east number 200 million, not counting those of the antichrist, and other world leaders, so they will need different modes of transport. So it could be just as John and Ezekiel saw it, men riding horses with perhaps guns and swords in their hands, only time will tell.

During this coming war, just before the attack of China and the other countries of the kings of the east upon Israel, the Euphrates

River will be removed as being an obstacle by being dried up. This will permit the march of the 200 million man army to reach the Valley of Jehoshaphat (Armageddon) just before Christ returns to fight against them (Rev. 9:16). There will also be other armies of the world gathered too, for John said there will be other world leaders. For all will be interested in Jerusalem. I should point out that prior to this gathering of armies in the Valley of Jehoshaphat (Armageddon), the antichrist will be opposed by other armies and will therefore be involved in conflicts and wars from the very beginning of his reign. As early as about a year after his rise, just prior to the first half of the Week, he will attack Egypt, according to Dan. 11:24 d-25. This will likely happen after his takeover of the formed ten nation confederacy, and from which he will take over (uproot) three of the countries. Now from the time of the Abomination, v31, and into the second half of the Week, there will be more wars. From Dan. 11:40-44, it clearly shows the antichrist being attacked by Egypt (King of the South) again, and he responding mightily. He will also attack and take over many other countries, with only Jordan escaping from his control. The peoples of Biblical Edom, Moab & Ammon are people all within the country of present day Jordan. Prophecy writers believe that the Jews will flee to Petra in Jordan, from the antichrist before, and after the Abomination. Daniel states that the Libyans and the Ethiopians shall be at his steps, meaning they will join with the antichrist in his war on Israel. The same nations are with Gog (antichrist) in the Ezekiel 39 prophecy.

Interestingly, while the kings of the east are marching towards the Euphrates, having already destroyed the antichrist's military headquarters in Iraq (could be a revived Babylon/Mosul?), things are happening simultaneously in Jerusalem. The city would have been under the prophetic/miraculous influence of the two witnesses who will by their miracles harass the antichrist's soldiers, as well as all who are not of the elect. This is now <u>after the tribulation</u>, with the 6th trumpet quickly following the 6th seal. The two witnesses (having finished their testimony), are captured and killed by the forces of the antichrist which are in Jerusalem. This 6th trumpet while also summoning the kings of the east to the Euphrates, also signals the death of the two witnesses and after three days of lying in the streets of Jerusalem, their resurrection to heaven, (Rev. 11:3-12). Here I'd like to say that it appears the two witnesses do live on after the tribulation, and also after the 6th seal, for here they are at the 6th trumpet, so their 1260 days end here, which means it would not have started at the same exact time of the 1260 days of the antichrist. This could be the difference which John hints at by saying "forty and two months" for the Gentiles, but said "a thousand two hundred and threescore days" with regards to the two witnesses. It seems to me that the great earthquake of the 6th seal does not significantly affect Jerusalem city, though it affects the islands and other lands of the world. For a great earthquake strikes Jerusalem, after the death of the two witnesses and their subsequent resurrection after 3 days, to heaven, vs. 13-14 states:

"**13 And the same hour was there a great earthquake, and the tenth part of the city [Jerusalem] fell, and in the earthquake were slain of men seven thousand: and the remnant were affrighted, and gave glory to the God of heaven. 14 The second woe is past; and, behold, the third woe cometh quickly.**

Then cometh the 6th plague. The plague dries up the river Euphrates at perhaps the very moment the army reaches its banks, or maybe just before, which allows the army to pass over on dry land. Up to this point, the kings of the east are bent on destroying the antichrist and his army, but the 6th plague draws them instead, to fight against Christ and His army in Israel. This is achieved by the seducing work of the three unclean frog-like spirits, which gather all the kings of the earth and of the whole world, to the battle of that great day of God Almighty. This will be the battle of Armageddon, set to take place in the Valley of Jehoshaphat. The 200 million army will take some time getting to Israel, where the antichrist and his army already awaits. The army has to go through the rest of western Iraq, then through Jordan and/or Syria, before getting to the Israeli theatre. The kings of the east could also be inclusive of India, Japan and Pakistan, etc..., while Russia from the north will also come. Still yet, there will be other nation armies joining the battle, for they will be drawn by the spirits of devils. Therefore, a grand march towards Jerusalem is happening here, as Zechariah said, "**And in that day will I make Jerusalem a burdensome stone for all people: all that burden themselves with it shall be cut in pieces, though all the people of the earth be gathered together against it." Zech. 12:3.**

However, the armies will not get to reach Jerusalem, but instead will reach the Valley of Jehoshaphat, for the battle of Armageddon. Here's how Zechariah saw the utter defeat of the armies:

[3] **Then shall the Lord go forth, and fight against those nations, as when he fought in the day of battle. [4] And his feet shall stand in that day upon the mount of Olives, which is before Jerusalem on the east, and the mount of Olives shall cleave in the midst thereof toward the east and toward the west, and there shall be a very great valley; and half of the mountain shall remove toward the north, and half of it toward the south.**

[12] **And this shall be the plague wherewith the Lord will smite all the people that have fought against Jerusalem; Their flesh shall consume away while they stand upon their feet, and their eyes shall consume away in their holes, and their tongue shall consume away in their mouth. [13] And it shall come to pass in that day, that a great tumult from the Lord shall be among them; and they shall lay hold every one on the hand of his neighbour, and his hand shall rise up against the hand of his neighbour. Zech. 14:3-4 & 12-13.**

So God gives each of Zechariah, Ezekiel, John and other prophets, different and sometimes similar details to this impending war of Armageddon. It's for us to study to show ourselves approved, to rightly divide the words, and thus receive the proper understanding thereof. The time draws closer to the end of the age, "**So likewise ye, when ye shall see all these things, know that it is near, even at the doors." Matt. 24:33.**

Then cometh the 7th seal. At its opening, silence ensues in heaven for about half an hour. John relates this using earthly time, as this is the best way he can express this. I do not believe time exists in Heaven, at least as we know time to be here on earth, for God dwells in eternity and time is only a slice out of eternity. This silence I believe is the prelude to the sounding of the 7th trumpet for the rapture of God's elect, so the angels wait in silent expectancy for God to give the command to blow the 7th and last trumpet. I believe it will be Michael, the arch-angel, who will sound this trumpet, for he is the war angel. Daniel 12 tells that "**at that time shall Michael stand up**" and God's people would be delivered, everyone found written in the book, surely this is at the rapture. It is clear the rapture has not taken place yet as we see an angel with much incense (Rev. 8), with the prayers of all saints being offered before God. This would surely not be so if the saints were already raptured. No one, angel or man, knows when God will give the command, only God knows, but the angels at this time knows it is imminent. So too will God's elect who are watchful and ready here on earth, but the angels have an armchair view, so to speak, they are in God's immediate presence after all.

THEN COMETH THE BIG MOMENT...THE COMMAND IS GIVEN, AND MICHAEL BLOWS THE 7TH AND LAST TRUMPET.

This is the moment that all creation has been waiting for; that the saints of God have been eagerly waiting for, from Adam to the present, and that God's enemies will all dread. Just prior to this trumpet, people will be eating and drinking, giving and partaking in marriage (the Gospels), and of course being involved in wars. Many will be taken by surprise, yes indeed. In fact, war is right there in Israel, but God is about to decisively put an end to man's rebellious nature. Paul said "behold, I shew you a mystery", and John states, "the mystery of God should be finished", and here both scriptures connect and end. The trumpet sounds, and the kingdoms of this world become the kingdoms of the Lord Jesus Christ, the angels of God are commanded to go to the four corners of the earth to gather God's elect (Gospels). The dead in Christ rise first, then all the elect who are still alive, will also rise up to meet the Lord in the air. The lord does not come down to earth yet, but his appearance is clearly seen, for **"Behold, he cometh with clouds; and every eye shall see him", see also Matt. 24.** HE steps on earth at Mount Olive at the 7th plague. In the meantime, while the world tries to come to grips with those taken from off the earth, while the armies are chomping at the bit for war at Armageddon, the elect goes up to the marriage supper of the Lamb. The 45 days after the tribulation are up, but I believe not a single man on earth will be able to know what day or date it is, due to the many cosmic disturbances that would have affected the whole solar system. Only the Lord God knows the time, day and hour of time.

After the rapture, the elect goes to the marriage supper of the Lamb, where they will receive their rewards. Rev. 19 tells the story of the aftermath of the 7th trumpet (the rapture), and then goes on to tell of the 7th plague. Here is the marriage supper:

Let us be glad and rejoice, and give honour to him: for the marriage of the Lamb is come, and his wife hath made herself ready. ^{8} And to her was granted that she should be arrayed in fine linen, clean and white: for the fine linen is the righteousness of saints. ^{9} And he saith unto me, Write, Blessed are they which are called unto the marriage supper of the Lamb. And he saith unto me, These are the true sayings of God. Rev. 19:7-9.

Recall that this is what Daniel stated in chapter 12, that **blessed** is he who waiteth and cometh to the 1335 days. Here John states, **blessed** are they which are called to the marriage supper of the Lamb. Thus the saints are gathered in heaven, where they will receive their rewards from the Lord. The rewards could be akin to such as those in the Gospels, like the parable of the talents of gold, etc., in Matt. 25. Of course, after the Millennium, the elect will also be able to enter the New Jerusalem (Rev. 21).

Here are further details on the aftermath of the rapture of the Elect in **Rev. 14.**

⁹ After this I beheld, and, lo, a great multitude, which no man could number, of all nations, and kindreds, and people, and tongues, stood before the throne, and before the Lamb, clothed with white robes, and palms in their hands;¹⁰ And cried with a loud voice, saying, Salvation to our God which sitteth upon the throne, and unto the Lamb.¹¹ And all the angels stood round about the throne, and about the elders and the four beasts, and fell before the throne on their faces, and worshipped God,¹² Saying, Amen: Blessing, and glory, and wisdom, and thanksgiving, and honour, and power, and might, be unto our God for ever and ever. Amen.¹³ And one of the elders answered, saying unto me, What are these which are arrayed in white robes? and whence came they?¹⁴ And I said unto him, Sir, thou knowest. And he said to me, These are they which came out of great tribulation, and have washed their robes, and made them white in the blood of the Lamb.¹⁵ Therefore are they before the throne of God, and serve him day and night in his temple: and he that sitteth on the throne shall dwell among them.¹⁶ They shall hunger no more, neither thirst any more; neither shall the sun light on them, nor any heat.¹⁷ For the Lamb which is in the midst of the throne shall feed them, and shall lead them unto living fountains of waters: and God shall wipe away all tears from their eyes. See also Rev. 19:7-9.

At the same time the elect is in heaven being rewarded, things are occurring on earth. The kings of the east have now completed their approximately 400 mile journey from the Euphrates to the Valley of Jehoshaphat. Only at the end will we know the various modes of transport they use, whether by foot, horses, tanks, planes, et cetera. There will be other armies of the world, that of the antichrist also, who will march to the Plain of Meggido. All will be gathered to the battle of the great day of the Lord. The time between the rapture & marriage supper (7ᵗʰ trumpet), and the wrath of God on the armies of the world at the 7ᵗʰ plague, must be short indeed. Since all who are raptured will be like the angels (spirit beings), then the supper and rewards are a supernatural event, which said thing can occur at speed unknown to the natural man. Therefore it could be mere hours or a day/s between events. The Bible refers to both events as occurring on the day of the Lord (2 Thess.), so I believe it's the same day, thus I lean to hours between events. After the marriage supper, the armies on earth see Christ and his armies appearing for the battle. Let's read:

¹¹ And I saw heaven opened, and behold a white horse; and he that sat upon him was called Faithful and True, and in righteousness he doth judge and make war. ¹² His eyes were as a flame of fire, and on his head were many crowns; and he had a name written, that no man knew, but he himself. ¹³ And he was clothed with a vesture dipped in blood: and his name is called The Word of God.

¹⁴ And the armies which were in heaven followed him upon white horses, clothed in fine linen, white and clean. ¹⁵ And out of his mouth goeth a sharp sword, that with it he should smite the nations: and he shall rule them with a rod of iron: and he treadeth the winepress of the fierceness and wrath of Almighty God. Rev.19.

The armies of the north, of the kings of the east and of the rest of the world, started out in opposition to the antichrist at first. However, due to the seductive influence of the spirits of devils, they all join together to oppose Christ, hence by the time they reach the Valley of Jehoshaphat / Plain of Meggido, they all have one mind (twisted as it is) to fight against Christ. This is of course an impossible task, for, can a man fight God and win? No, I tell you, it's impossible to defeat God, but in their twisted and hate-filled mind, and their numbers, they become confident. Their utter defeat is swift! Ezek. 39, Rev. 19, Zechariah, Daniel and Isaiah in various ways, tell the story of their doom. I have discussed some of these before. They turn and slay one another, and they are buffeted by God's great hailstones, weighing approx. 64 pounds, thunder and lightnings. It is utter chaos, confusion and carnage among their ranks. John saw their blood flowing up to the horses bridles (approx. 5-6 ft) for 200 miles. Wow!!! Blink and read again! And believe it. See Rev. 14 below:

¹⁹ And the angel thrust in his sickle into the earth, and gathered the vine of the earth, and cast it into the great winepress of the wrath of God. ²⁰ And the winepress was trodden without the city, and blood came out of the winepress, even unto the horse bridles, by the space of a thousand and six hundred furlongs. Rev. 14.

The Jews spend 7 years collecting and burning the spoils of war, and burying the dead for 7 months, according to Ezekiel 39. This story could imply that it really will be olden days type weapons that will be used in this war, or it could be Ezekiel using old time terminologies like John to describe the war. If this will be the case, then some drastic changes would have taken place on earth by then to cause this situation. This is not impossible, for the many cosmic disturbances, the earthquakes and subsequent land movements of the 6th seal among other happenings, could very well cause a destruction of many of today's modern weapons, such as tanks, helicopters/planes, and nuclear weapons. This would cause a return to the use of ancient weapons, such as swords, time will tell, but the war will certainly occur, for thus saith the Lord. This then leaves me to discuss the matter of the timing of the seals-trumpets-plagues as they relate to the 70th Week and some other matters.

5 The Timing of Some Events

The antichrist

The rise of the antichrist must take place before the Week begins, but the world will not see him as such, until the Abomination of Desolation is set up. As a matter of fact, only the people who know the prophecy will know then that it is the antichrist they are looking at. The world at large will still not know until at 1260 days when he proclaims himself as God, then it will be too late for many to switch allegiance from him. I believe he is around right now, in the waiting though, until his appointed time. He will rise after the Ten Nation Ottoman Islamic Kingdom is set up, which by some trickery, he will take over as leader. He will take over a new nation that will be formed right amongst the ten, that is, within their borders. This new nation will seek and gain independence from within the borders of the ten. It will in all likelihood, be supported in its drive for independence, by the United Nations, NATO, the European Union, the United States and Russia. This may involve some amount of bloodshed by various ethnic groups, example the Kurds, fighting for their independence. The antichrist will stay in the background directing the fight, and will conveniently be elected leader once the independence is achieved. As stated above, he will then through subtlety and trickery, rise up to lead and take control of the Ten Nation Ottoman Islamic Kingdom. For he will not be given the honour of the Kingdom by regular means.

After he takes over and begin to attack other countries, he may not appear to be the one actively fighting against the countries, and may stay in the background directing the moves and subsequent takeovers as he expands. He will then set up his own sub-commanders to lead these and other countries that he will overtake and conquer. I believe he will appear to be peaceful and loving at first (first 3 ½ yrs), but his nature is evil, thus it will not last for long. From the very beginning, aspects of his true nature will show, but only those who know the prophecies will see him for what he is. Others will simply choose to look the other way and trumpet his good deeds, much like they did with Hitler, until his true nature came to the fore, then it was too late. This will allow him to rise almost unopposed, due to his use of flattery and deceit. I believe he will show his face on the world stage, immediately or within a few years (1-3) after the Middle East War of Psalm 83. He will not be the antichrist then, only a man of evil proportions, and only at the 30 day point after the Abomination of Desolation will he assume that role, when he will be inhabited directly by satan. At the start of the final 1260 days, the false prophet will announce him as God and order that a statue of him be built and worshipped. He may even be referred to as the Muslim Mahdi at that point. The rest as they say, will be history, except that God has already spoken of what will occur, before it occurs. After he becomes the antichrist, he will through the mark of the beast, cause many people to be killed except they take the mark.

The seals-trumpets-plagues

The way the order of the seals-trumpets-plagues of Revelation are set up, would seem to suggest that they begin soon after the Abomination has been set up. They will therefore run the course of the second half of the Week, 1260 days, and until Armageddon. Conversely, they may start, at some time just prior to the Middle of the Week. I believe though that they start at the Middle of the Week, for the antichrist is given his crown from the 1st seal, and he went forth conquering and to conquer, and he is given 42 months/1260 days to reign. This must be after the Abomination (after 30 days), when he will set up himself as God in the Temple. Notice that by the 1st plague, the mark of the beast is already upon men, for a grievous sore fell upon them that had the mark. The mark of the beast may have begun to be given from within the latter part of the first half of the Week (last 30 days?), with this though being an optional requirement. However, I believe it will become mandatory after the Abomination has been set up, during the last 30 days of the first part of the Week, and the beast will then require the earth to worship him as God. This will cause the betrayal of many Christians and others who reject the mark, by those who accept the mark, betraying their own family members and friends to the antichrist. See Matt. 24, where Jesus points this out. For one cannot buy or sell except he/she has the mark, so many will sell out to the antichrist, especially as they will believe that he is God.

The 144 000

The sealing of the 144,000 Jews of Israel is first mentioned in Rev. 7, then some more details are given in Rev. 14. The sealing has to occur before the Abomination, or very soon after, since the grievous sore fell upon the men who has the mark of the beast, and that worship his image, from within the first of the triplet system (1st plague). The image will be set up after the Abomination (after 30 days), but know that the image and the Abomination could be one and the same thing. By the time of the sounding of the 5th trumpet, the locusts were commanded to only hurt those men that had not the seal of God in their foreheads. This therefore alludes to the fact that God's chosen people, the elect, were already sealed by God. As a matter of fact the Word of God states: "**Nevertheless the foundation of God standeth sure, having this seal, the Lord knoweth them that are his**", **2 Tim. 2:19**. Not only that, but God also said, "**According as he hath chosen us in him before the foundation of the world, that we should be holy and without blame before him in love:**" So God always know those that are his, for HE KNOWS ALL THINGS, and there is never a time when God does not know all things. So for me, a child of God will be sealed from he/she is born again, for the Lord already knows all who will be ready to meet HIM at HIS appearing.

Mystery Babylon and the false prophet

Where is mystery Babylon? This question has been poured over by many prophecy writers, with varying answers given. The timing of its burning and utter destruction is more important here to me. I believe because she is attacked by the ten kings that reign for one hour (30 days?) with the beast, then this is perhaps up to or within the 30 days after the Abomination. Why do I say this? The beast rises amongst the ten, who then reign with him for an hour, but as soon as he becomes the beast/antichrist, that is, when his official reign begins, he will uproot three nations. They perhaps do not agree with his agenda, so he uproots the three (removes three leaders/kings), which leaves him with 7 nations, with a king ruled by him. **The beast's official reign (1260 days) will begin 30 days after he sets up the Abomination, which will be 1260 days/42 months from there to the ending of his reign (see Time-line chart).** For he will not be seen to be the beast in the first half of the Week, as the world will wonder after the beast and follow him. It is at the Middle of the Week, at 1260 days (1230+30) that people will be forced/commanded to worship the beast and his image. So the ten kings (nations), with the authority of the antichrist, will attack the whore within this 30 day window. Here's John take on it.

And the ten horns which thou sawest upon the beast, these shall hate the whore, and shall make her desolate and naked, and shall eat her flesh, and burn her with fire. Rev. 17:16.

Some prophecy writers label Rome as mystery Babylon and they may be right. For the original Babylon, though having killed many of God's people, is disqualified because it is not built on 7 hills (mountains), but Rome as a city is. Rome, quite knowingly, from a little before the time of Christ, while under the auspices of the Roman Empire, has slaughtered millions of Christians. Though original Babylon I believe will be revived, in the form of the Ottoman Islamic Empire (an Islamic Caliphate), I lean towards Rome being the city that is called mystery Babylon. This therefore could make the Pope, the false prophet, something which is quite plausible. For the Pope at this time is busy making overtures to the Muslims of the Middle East, in trying to bring all religions together as one. If the Pope is the false prophet, sometime after the rise of the antichrist, the Pope will then assume his position as that of the false prophet. He will join forces with the antichrist, as he will be tricked or coerced into becoming a mouthpiece for the antichrist. He will, as Pope, hold a significant sway over the world, even enticing them to worship the beast and the image of the beast. The Pope already holds a tremendous sway over the Christian world, with the Catholic Church allowing Priests to accept and forgive confession of sins given by its constituents. Therefore, the man who is Pope at that time, would certainly maintain the status quo. But what a travesty? Behold, only the Almighty God, can and is able to forgive sins as it relates to salvation, through the death, burial and resurrection of Jesus Christ.

Conversely, the false prophet could be a Muslim Cleric, Scholar or an Imam, or a possessor of all these offices, of Jewish heritage, and well beloved and esteemed by the Muslim world. Why do I say this? Apostle John in Revelation 13, said that the beast arises from the sea, but that the false prophet arises after, however, he rises from the earth. In scripture, the sea is representative of the Gentile nations, from which all the leaders of the previous seven world empires came, and from which the beast, the 8th, will come. However, John saw the false prophet rising from the earth or (the land), which refers to the land of Israel. So the false prophet will be an Apostate Jew, or one who abandons the Torah, perhaps for the Koran. Notice he has horns like a lamb but with a voice of a dragon. This means he will appear harmless and loveable to people, but when he speaks, it will be with evil intentions. Later on in Rev., the beast entity, that is, the beast and the ten leaders, attack the whore, which I believe is Rome. It stands to reason therefore, that the false prophet may not be a Pope, since firstly, Popes have been established since at least A.D. 90, and secondly, Rome being destroyed would not therefore produce the false prophet, who will likely be killed by then. Unless by virtue of Rome's destruction, as said above, the Pope is coerced into becoming the false prophet, but I am holding to the false prophet not being a Pope. On the other hand, an Imam could arise to become a world authority, espousing the antichrist as God to the world. Time will tell, as God has not expressly say who it is, but at the time of the end, such matters will become clear.

To continue the thought on Rome as mystery Babylon though, it is still not far-fetched to think it could be the original city area of Babylon, for the kings of the east will destroy the antichrist's Military HQ. Said HQ will be in Iraq, possibly the Nineveh/Mosul area, which ISIS controls (at time of writing), an area I predict the antichrist will eventually control. This Mosul is right across from where Babylon is, in Nineveh province in Iraq. That is, Nineveh is on the west side of the river Tigris from Mosul which is on the east side. So it could be the original Babylon, however, time will tell. It IS NOT the USA though, as some posit, for USA is a country, and John specifically said the whore is a city. Rev. 14, 17 & 18 tell the story of Babylon, the whore of the earth. John Preacher in his book, The Islamic Antichrist, labels Saudi Arabia, which has Mecca and Medina (Islamic holy sites), as the whore, due to its oil and other wealth that it sells to the world. He believes that this nation is mystery Babylon. However, Saudi Arabia is a country, not a city as is mystery Babylon, so Rome seems perfectly suited to be that city. Like I said though, time will tell.

The mark of the Beast

Many have speculated on what this actual mark could be. Some have said it is the Roman numerals seen on the Pontiff's mitre, that add up to 666. Yet others have come up with other ideas. But I think highly of John Preacher's idea that it has to with some Muslim writings that equate to the same 666. I have already stated earlier, that the next kingdom will be an Islamic kingdom, the 8th (Antichrist) which is of the 7th (Ottoman). The culture of Islam is one which is replete with its followers using headgear, scarfs, flags, etc, with certain writings on them. The symbols of the Bismillah (seen below), the symbol of the crossed swords, and the star and crescent moon are all popular (refer back to the map and flag of the Ottoman Islamic Empire). See also the book by John Preacher, The Islamic Antichrist, especially the chapter on "the mark of the beast", an impressive book I believe. It seems likely therefore, that since the kingdom is Islamic, then reason dictates that the symbols will include some or all of the above, but will definitely equate numerically to 666. **I believe this mark is literal, for the way it is expressly written by Apostle John. This 666, which the symbol/s will add up to, will be placed in the forehead and on the right hand, in the form of a permanent stamp, exactly as John foresaw.**

I do not know whether this may turn out to be computerized chip as is already on the scene in some countries, and is fully in use on animals. The chip will be difficult to be seen though (said to be small as a rice grain) and John seemed expressly to be saying, that the mark can be readily seen. Still, some humans have actually accepted the chip on their bodies, so you can see that it will not be too difficult to convince people that the chip or the mark will be beneficial to their well-being. Do note however, that the consequences for all who take the mark, whether willingly or even after torture, is seen in Rev. 14:9-11 & 16:2. The destiny is eternal hell, for all who take the mark, there is no escape from the judgement of hell and damnation, as given by God.

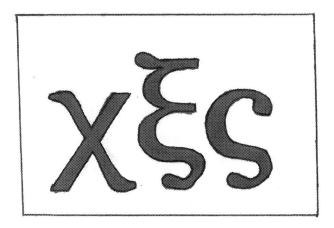

This is reputed to actually count up to exactly 666, coming from the Greek letters Chi Xi Stigma, which spells the Arabic word in Islam, the Bismillah. This I believe, is the mark of the beast.

The Millennium

The Millennium is the 1000 years of Christ rule on earth after the fires of Armageddon. In fact, the Jews will go seven (7) years into the Millennium burning the weapons of war from the battle of Armageddon, according to Ezekiel 39. The new Temple will be built and consecrated (Ezek. 40-43), and God will be King over all the earth, and HIS name shall be one, and there shall be one Lord. The nations of the earth will have to go up to Jerusalem yearly to worship the Lord God Almighty, to keep the feast of tabernacles and will receive no rain upon them, should they fail to do so. Satan, the old dragon, yes, will be bound for the said thousand years, thus people will be free of his tempting and seducing ways. All the people of

God from Adam right up to Jesus' 2nd return, who are raptured, will live and reign with HIM, for the thousand years. All the dead from Adam to Jesus' 2nd return, who never served Christ as Lord and Saviour, will remain dead throughout the thousand years. This is the first resurrection. The second death has no power over them (the raptured), who make it in the first resurrection.

However, after the thousand years (Millennium) have expired, satan, true to his deceiving nature, as soon as he is released as per the will of God, he immediately returns to his lying and destructive ways. As the spirit of Gog, he will go to the four quarters of the earth and deceive the nations for one last battle with the Lord. Having not endured temptation for a thousand years, the people quickly and easily join with the devil. They surround the beloved city of Jerusalem, but the fire of God destroys them all ...... **"And the devil that deceived them was cast into the lake of fire and brimstone, where the beast and the false prophet are, and shall be tormented day and night for ever and ever".** Rev. 20:10. Then cometh the great white throne judgement where all the dead, that is, all the remaining dead who were not raptured, and those who the devil deceive in the 2nd Gog war, now all stand before God to be judged. Here is the judgement scene.

[12] And I saw the dead, small and great, stand before God; and the books were opened: and another book was opened, which is the book of life: and the dead were judged out of those things which were written in the books, according to their works.

[13] And the sea gave up the dead which were in it; and death and hell delivered up the dead which were in them: and they were judged every man according to their works. [14] And death and hell were cast into the lake of fire. This is the second death. [15] And whosoever was not found written in the book of life was cast into the lake of fire. Rev. 20:12-15.

After this judgement, (called the Great White Throne Judgement) is over, God produces a new heaven and a new earth, that has no sea; this is unlike our earth today which has so many seas, for example, the Caribbean Sea. HE sends down the New Jerusalem, prepared for

HIS people, and they live for evermore with God. John puts it like this:

⁴ And God shall wipe away all tears from their eyes; and there shall be no more death, neither sorrow, nor crying, neither shall there be any more pain: for the former things are passed away. Rev. 21:4.

Daniel 11: 21-45 - Explanation

Daniel chapter 11 gives a huge foretelling of the antichrist's rise to power, from just prior to the start of the Week, his actions in the first and second half of the Week, and then his eventual death at Armageddon. Daniel gives an overview of the actions of the various Kings of the North (Seleucid) in their wars against the Kings of the South (Ptolemy) in this chapter. From verse 3, he told the story of Alexander the Great's rise and fall, and the subsequent breakup of his kingdom into four smaller kingdoms which were ruled by his four generals. Eventually, two of the generals became powerful enough to become the Seleucid and the Ptolemy Kingdoms, which were ruled by various leaders over time. From verse 21 onwards though, he is definitely speaking of the future antichrist, and not Antiochus Epiphanes as many believe. Although Antiochus did some terrible things to the Jews, he by no means accomplished the tremendous feats tabled here by Daniel. I will show the scriptural text first and then give the explanation.

The period before, and up to the first half of the Week – first 3 ½ yrs

²¹ And in his estate shall stand up a vile person, to whom they shall not give the honour of the kingdom: but he shall come in peaceably, and obtain the kingdom by flatteries. ²² And with the arms of a flood shall they be overflown from before him, and shall be broken; yea, also the prince of the covenant. ²³ And after the league made with him he shall work deceitfully: for he shall come up, and shall become strong with a small people. <u>Dan. 21: 21-24.</u>

Here we see that a long period of time between vs. 20 and 21, has taken place, time spanning from the last king of the Seleucid Empire to the present. In fact at the time of writing (2015), I SAY THAT THIS HAS NOT YET OCCURRED, that is, the arrival of this "vile person" has not yet occurred. So this is clearly a break in the action as Daniel was giving here. Thus, after the death of this King of the North, Daniel jumps right to the time of the end. So even though Antiochus did some of the things here, like attack Egypt, and in 168 B.C. defiled the Jewish Temple by offering a pig on the Altar, killed many Jews and burnt many Scriptures, enslaved many Jews, etc., this text is all about the coming man of sin. The antichrist as stated before, comes on the scene with a new country near the time of the end, as a supposedly peaceful ruler. This will occur right near the time when the nation of Israel will be attacked by a confederacy of Middle East nations, as per Psalm 83, see chap. 2. Interestingly, the rise of the new nation with the antichrist may not be given adequate news coverage around the world, due to the impending and actual war of Psalm 83. Almost all world attention will be centered on this war, and as such the rise of the new nation with the antichrist person, will hardly be noticed. The new nation will rise up in spite of there being a ten nation Islamic kingdom confederacy controlling the said land space that the new country will arise in. For it will arise among the ten. He then sets about by covert means to become ruler of the ten, but the leadership of the kingdom will not be given to him by fair and regular means, thus his recourse to covert, flattering and deceitful means to accomplish his goal.

The antichrist will easily overcome the leaders of the ten nation kingdom, even the chief leader of the ten. For they shall be broken, which suggests that he will possess superior skills and weaponry, and make spectacular boasts to them, such that they simple accede to him as their leader. Thus an agreement will be made with him by the ten leaders, perhaps said agreement (covenant with the many), being the complete capture of Israel and its capital Jerusalem and its return to Muslim hands after their defeat by Israel (Psa. 83 war, see chap 2).

This I believe refers to Dan. 9:27, **"And he shall confirm the covenant with many for one week:"** He will also promise them the world, said trick that satan tried with Jesus Christ before. He will promise a complete Muslim control of world affairs, with their religion becoming the dominant and perhaps the only recognized religion in the world. But of course, he will only be deceiving them, for he will work deceitfully, as the antichrist will not regard any god and will only recognize the god of forces. However, he will play along with the Muslims, allowing them freedom in so far as it accomplishes his plans, until the appointed time when he betrays them and exalts himself as God and demands that he be worshipped.

24 He shall enter peaceably even upon the fattest places of the province; and he shall do that which his fathers have not done, nor his fathers' fathers; he shall scatter among them the prey, and spoil, and riches: yea, and he shall forecast his devices against the strong holds, even for a time. 25 And he shall stir up his power and his courage against the king of the south with a great army; and the king of the south shall be stirred up to battle with a very great and mighty army; but he shall not stand: for they shall forecast devices against him.

26 Yea, they that feed of the portion of his meat shall destroy him, and his army shall overflow: and many shall fall down slain. 27 And both of these kings' hearts shall be to do mischief, and they shall speak lies at one table; but it shall not prosper: for yet the end shall be at the time appointed. 28 Then shall he return into his land with great riches; and his heart shall be against the holy covenant; and he shall do exploits, and return to his own land.

29 At the time appointed he shall return, and come toward the south; but it shall not be as the former, or as the latter. 30 For the ships of Chittim shall come against him: therefore he shall be grieved, and return, and have indignation against the holy covenant: so shall he do; he shall even return, and have intelligence with them that forsake the holy covenant. 31 And arms shall stand on his part, and they shall pollute the sanctuary of strength, and shall take away the daily sacrifice, and they shall place the abomination that maketh desolate. <u>Dan. 11:21-31</u>

Before he becomes the antichrist, he will provide plenty of wealth and substance to the Muslim partners, perhaps from oil, as he will suddenly be in complete control of a lot oil fields. He will therefore do the opposite to what his forefathers had done, that is, he will share the wealth around among his Muslim partners, and many shall be enriched. He will make plans to attack and capture other countries, and will set the pieces in motion. All this will happen within one to two years after him gaining control over the ten nation's confederacy. Then he will attack Egypt (King of the South), with a large army, as he will now be in charge of a single integrated defense force, comprised from all the ten nations. The King of Egypt will respond with a large army likewise, but his own people shall betray him and his army shall be utterly defeated. Then the antichrist and the king (leader) of Egypt will meet at a table to make peace, but both will be lying to the other. For their secret intention will be to destroy the other. After the meeting, the antichrist will return to his own country with many of the riches of Egypt.

On his way back to his country via the Mediterranean Sea, hinted at by his second return (vs.29-30), the antichrist's heart will be set against the Holy Covenant of the Jews. This covenant is between God and the Jews, where the Jews were called out and set apart as a distinct and peculiar people with their own religion – Judaism - with its own laws, rituals and ordinances, distinct from all other religions. This especially occurred from the time of Moses, who was eventually called up to Mount Sinai and given the Law of 10 Commandments which were a summary of the full 613 Commandments. This is the Holy Covenant. Do note however, that Abraham is the father of the nation of Israel, as he was the first one called out by God from among his kindred, and along with Sarah, procreated and started the nation of Israel. The antichrist will take some action against the Holy Covenant but I do not see him attacking Israel at this time. The time is not yet right, so he may instead resort to some underhand means to prepare the way for his real attack, example spy out the locale. He may also form friendships with some deceitful Jews or radical Palestinians like Hamas, who will later betray and aid in his future march on Israel. Then he continues his journey home, which is perhaps straddling the borders of Turkey, Syria, and Iraq.

At a later date, perhaps nearer to the 3 year point of the first half of the Week, the antichrist decides to re-attack Egypt. This time however, perhaps his third attack on Egypt, he will encounter resistance, in the form of naval forces coming from the island of Chittim. This island is said to be Cyprus, Chittim being the old name, and it is perfectly situated in the Mediterranean Sea (see Middle East maps) to so apply pressure to the antichrist forces. There is a country with two naval bases on the island, the United Kingdom, who maintains a military presence on the western side of the island in order to keep a strategic location in the eastern Mediterranean Sea. It may be that Russia by that time will also have a base their, as the two countries currently have an agreement that allows the Russian Navy to dock warships at their ports for use as counter-terrorism and anti-piracy actions. So a future joint force acting against the antichrist ships seems to be what Daniel foresaw. The antichrist will be grieved, and this means he does not yet control the whole world. He may even feel betrayed by these European forces fighting from Cyprus and resisting his advance on Egypt. In fury, he turns back and then proceeds to act against the Holy Covenant. He will suddenly decide, along with his Muslim partners, to go and attack Jerusalem, Israel. Some deceitful Jews who side with the antichrist, may also be involved in setting up the attack on their own country, or these may be radical Muslims, for he will make plans ("have intelligence") with them. They will in turn be betrayed by the antichrist after he captures Jerusalem. See chapter 3 for the attack on Jerusalem in the Jerusalem War.

This war is set to take place at close to the end of the first half of the Week, 1160-1200 days. Thus he marches on Jerusalem, taking the route from Ai to Shufat and then unto Old Jerusalem, just after 3 years of the Week. He arrives at Jerusalem and meets resistance from the Jews who have blockaded themselves inside the city. The antichrist besieges the city for perhaps 40 days (the period of suffering), but he breaks through at the 1230 day point of the Week and proceeds to place the Abomination of Desolation. His forces will stand guard at the Temple Mount and will pollute the area by virtue of their atrocities, they will also stop the daily sacrifice of the Jews. From that point on (1230 days), the Jews will have 30 days to escape Jerusalem, but this will be easier said than done. For the antichrist's soldiers will be pillaging and killing those that are caught, but many will definitely escape his clutches and flee to Petra in Jordan. So there is Daniel's 1290 days to the end of the tribulation. After the 30 days are ended, the midway point of the Week (1260 days), will be reached, and the mandatory mark of the beast becomes effective. The antichrist proclaims himself as god in the Temple, and only then truly becomes the antichrist (taken over by the devil), the man of sin, or the son of perdition.

Before I go to the second half of the Week, let me make an important point here. The Abomination of Desolation that Daniel spoke about, which the antichrist sets up at 1230 days, clearly shows that he was not referring to Antiochus Epiphanes. Why do I say this? Firstly Antiochus was from a line of several successive Seleucid kings – the 8th of 17th – so the kingdom was already long established. The Seleucid region of Syria and its environs encompassing even Jerusalem was already there. On the other hand, the antichrist will rise to become the leader of **a new country** at the time of the end, and ultimately also lead the ten nations before he removes three of the kings of the ten. Secondly, recall that Jesus referred to the Abomination in the Gospels, example at Matt. 24:15, **"When ye therefore shall see the abomination of desolation…"**. Please note that Jesus referred to it in the future tense as well as drew the Apostles attention back to the Daniel text. A careful study of Jewish history will prove that this day and its subsequent related occurrences, have never before taken place, notwithstanding the various Temple destructions and desecrations. So unto the second half of the Week we go.

The second half of the Week – second 3 ½ years

[32] And such as do wickedly against the covenant shall he corrupt by flatteries: but the people that do know their God shall be strong, and do exploits. [33] And they that understand among the people shall instruct many: yet they shall fall by the sword, and by flame, by captivity, and by spoil, many days.

[34] Now when they shall fall, they shall be holpen with a little help: but many shall cleave to them with flatteries. [35] And some of them of understanding shall fall, to try them, and to purge, and to make them white, even to the time of the end: because it is yet for a time appointed. [36] And the king shall do according to his will; and he shall exalt himself, and magnify himself above every god, and shall speak marvellous things against the God of gods, and shall prosper till the indignation be accomplished: for that that is determined shall be done.

[37] Neither shall he regard the God of his fathers, nor the desire of women, nor regard any god: for he shall magnify himself above all. [38] But in his estate shall he honour the God of forces: and a god whom his fathers knew not shall he honour with gold, and silver, and with precious stones, and pleasant things. [39] Thus shall he do in the most strong holds with a strange god, whom he shall acknowledge and increase with glory: and he shall cause them to rule over many, and shall divide the land for gain.

[40] And at the time of the end shall the king of the south push at him: and the king of the north shall come against him like a whirlwind, with chariots, and with horsemen, and with many ships; and he shall enter into the countries, and shall overflow and pass over. [41] He shall enter also into the glorious land, and many countries shall be overthrown: but these shall escape out of his hand, even Edom, and Moab, and the chief of the children of Ammon. [42] He shall stretch forth his hand also upon the countries: and the land of Egypt shall not escape.

[43] But he shall have power over the treasures of gold and of silver, and over all the precious things of Egypt: and the Libyans and the Ethiopians shall be at his steps. [44] But tidings out of the east and out of the north shall trouble him: therefore he shall go forth with great fury to destroy, and utterly to make away many. [45] And he shall plant the tabernacles of his palace between the seas in the glorious holy mountain; yet he shall come to his end, and none shall help him. <u>Dan. 21: 31-45.</u>

The antichrist starts the second half of the Week with the Abomination of Desolation already in place for 30 days. He will corrupt by flatteries all those who are against the Holy Covenant. However, the true saints of God will not buckle and give in, or take his evil mark. Instead much like the three Hebrew men of Daniel's time, with Daniel himself being one of them, the true people of God will fight back and do wonders. I believe they will perform many miracles, really great miracles that God will empower them to do, so as to counteract the old dragon in the form of the antichrist. However, many saints will be caught and killed by the sword or burnt at the stake during this last 1260 days, preferring death than to join the antichrist. Many will be betrayed even by their own family and friends.

Meanwhile the antichrist will not always be at Jerusalem, but will go elsewhere in campaigning, for he will be a warmonger. He will make many boasts against the Lord God and seek to do his own will, and will continue until his appointed time of 1260 days are up. Due to his warmongering ways, he will not even have time for women in his life, neither will he regard any other god. He will be totally and completely self-conceited and self-centered, and will instead honour the god of war. He will give honour to this god with all types of precious stones, like gold and silver. He will put sub-commanders in charge of the countries captured and will divide the land of Israel for personal gain and to the Muslims.

Then he will re-attack Egypt and many other countries successfully, for who shall make war with the beast. However, interestingly, the country of Jordan escapes from him. Now Edom, Moab and Ammon were all cities and peoples within the land area now called Jordan. They were close relatives to the Jews through the lineage of Lot, Abraham's nehpew. Indeed the present capital of Jordan, which is Amman is at the site where the ancient capital of Ammon was, that is, Rabbath-ammon. Do note the spelling difference of ancient <u>Ammon</u> and present day <u>Amman</u>. Why does Jordan escape the antichrist? Seventy five (75%) of Jordan's current population is made up of Palestinians. Daniel says the "chief of the children of Ammon escapes", this seems to refer to the King of Jordan. Jordan's current ruler is king Abdullah II, he is a direct descendant of the prophet Mohammed, and is also of the Hashemite family which once controlled the Hashemite kingdom.

The antichrist will be regarded by Muslims as their prophesied Mahdi, so close family connections are what may cause the antichrist to leave the King of Jordan alone. The Lord also commanded the Jews to flee to the mountains when they see the Abomination and Jordan (Edom) will be right in their path. Rev. 12:13-16 says the antichrist will pursue the escaping Jews across the desert, but the earth will swallow the flood of water (soldiers) that the antichrist sends after them. The earth opens her mouth (an earthquake perhaps?) and swallows the flood and thus the Jews are supernaturally saved. Additionally, Isaiah 63 has the Lord coming from Bozrah which is in Edom, with his garments dyed red, suggesting the blood of the enemy that are killed. So for all these reasons, Jordan will escape the antichrist's hands.

The antichrist will capture Egypt, and all its wealth of gold, silver and precious artifacts, and the Libyans and the Ethiopians who may have sided/fought alongside Egypt, now become subservient to the antichrist. But then bad news comes from the east and north which will greatly trouble the antichrist. As said earlier, this shows that the antichrist is neither at Jerusalem, nor at his home-base in Iraq at the time, but perhaps in Egypt, Ethiopa or Libya. Therefore the kings of the east with their 200 million man army, will march on a revived Babylonian Ottoman Islamic Empire and destroy the capital before the antichrist can get back. This will signal the end of the antichrist's kingdom reign, that is, his 1260 day reign. His death though comes later at Armageddon. It seems also that the Russian army may also decide to attack the antichrist forces at Jerusalem at the same time, and as such the antichrist will be furious at these developments. He will return with a rage intending to destroy all before him, for he will not give up his kingdom that easily.

He gets back to Israel, gathers his forces and marches towards the plain of Megiddo intending to slaughter the two armies who are by then marching towards the same place. Before the war is enjoined, the rapture takes place and while the saints receive their rewards, the armies are seduced and made to join forces. The antichrist will make them believe that they can fight the armies of God and win, since he himself is a god. Then Christ returns with his heavenly army and causes such confusion among the armies of the antichrist, that they turn on each other and begin killing each other. God also rain down great hailstones on the armies, with lightning and thundering. The birds of the air are called upon to come and feast upon the flesh of men and of horses. This is the battle of Armageddon, which is the 7th plague. The antichrist is slain, along with the most of the earthly armies and the Jews on earth proceed to clean up all the way into the early part of the Millennium.

This is Daniel's 11 vision of the antichrist as given by the Lord God of heaven. That is my explanation according to my revelation and understanding thereof.

To God be the glory, the honour and the praise, Blessed be HE! May I be accounted worthy of the first resurrection.

Epilogue

This book was written over a period of several months, starting in early 2015 and was finished at year end or so I thought. But I was then inspired to add the final section of Daniel 11 explanation to chapter 5. An important addition I came to realize afterwards. I have touched on several sensitive topics that will have many readers thinking, 'no, that is incorrect!' But I will stand by them until if and when God shows me otherwise.

The vision of the man who will become the antichrist/beast, shown to me by the Lord God in the late 90s, was exceedingly powerful. I was made quite nervous and troubled at his picture whilst in the vision, yet it was only a dream. I was shown other visions also, which is how I came to understand many scriptures better. In them, I was taken forward in time and shown some of the future. Many church leaders preach the Pre-tribulation rapture, but I trust by now your eyes and thus your understanding will have been opened to the truth. To God be the glory for HIS revelations. Through HIM, I hope many others will be enlightened. Many will be shocked to see the antichrist on the scene, and they are yet here on earth, in spite of being fore-warned by the Bible, this book and by other writers. But he that shall endure unto the end, the same shall be saved.

The identity of the false prophet and the exact spot of land of the country of the antichrist, were not revealed to me by the Lord at the time of writing. However, other revelations and careful studying of related scriptures, allowed me to draw informed conclusions. Thus I am confident with the said conclusions, and I have carefully laid out my reasons. One such example is the origins of the antichrist being a Middle Eastern person or of Middle Eastern heritage, in chapter 2. I also came to the conclusion of the Ottoman Empire as being the 7th after many years of studying. From that conclusion, much more understanding came to me. To God be the glory, blessed be HE.

Do share this information with others, so that they may be prepared to face the terrible coming time of the last and 70th Week, especially the last 3 ½ years – the Great Tribulation. Only in Daniel 11, do we see the full 7 years of the antichrist from his rise to his death. All other Bible writers only give parts of his actions, but they are nonetheless very important to the overall picture. God never reveals everything to us humans all at once, it would probably mad us. Careful studying and researching is needed, guided by the Spirit of course. This is a great piece of writing by Daniel, to have captured it so precisely in such an abbreviated format, surely this is the Hand of God. Jesus said, "And except those days should be shortened, there should no flesh be saved: but for the elect's sake those days shall be shortened."[limited].

I am a One God, Apostolic Christian, Holy Ghost filled, tongues talking (glossolalia) too. It will take the Holy Ghost to quicken (change) our mortal bodies to immortality, to rise up and meet our Saviour in the air. **You must be born again, as Jesus said in St. John 3**. I am a believer in the Acts 2:38 doctrine of Jesus Christ. Yes, I am baptized in the name of the Lord Jesus Christ. The LORD bless thee, and keep thee: The LORD make his face shine upon thee, and be gracious unto thee: The LORD lift up his countenance upon thee, and give thee peace. In Jesus' name, Amen!

I pray for the peace of Jerusalem.

Bibliography

Web. http://www.Therapture/en.Wikipedia.org

The Bible, 1611 King James Version

Strong, James, S.T.D., LL.D., Strong Exhaustive Concordance Bible, Updated Edition

Web. http://www.en.wikipedia.org/wiki/File:OttomanEmpireIn1683.png

Web. http://www.en.wikipedia.org/wiki/Antiochus_iv_Epiphanes

Web. The Jewish Press.com

Web. http://www.tribwatch.com/updateIraqIndex.htm

Preacher, John,The Islamic Antichrist.

The Bible, New International Version

Printed in the United States
By Bookmasters